'The subject of this book is nothing less than "the necessity" and problematics "of seeking truth" as analysts confront the vital enigmas of the human mind and attempt to articulate and address the problems to which they give rise. It is not only an important explication of the contributions of a remarkable analyst, but it is a remarkable book by a remarkable author, one that should prove essential reading to clinicians at all levels as they struggle to engage with and create the psychoanalysis of the 21st century.'

Howard B. Levine, *Editor-in-chief,*
The Routledge W.R. Bion Studies series.

'Steven Jaron's moving account of his work with his patients, with Christopher Bollas as his theoretical and psychic guide, gives the lay reader a touching insight into how the psychoanalytic process can bring compassion and healing. Bollas's work to uncover the mostly hidden, in the form of the unthought known, is given historical and emotional background in Jaron's thoughtful book whose starting point is the search for reverie in Bollas—the analyst as a seer, a feeling observer of our shadow selves.'

Anish Kapoor

Christopher Bollas

This book provides a clear and accessible overview of the seminal clinical thinking of Christopher Bollas.

Placing Bollas's writings besides those of analysts including Milner, Bion, Winnicott, Lacan and Green, Steven Jaron examines the central concept of the unthought known in terms of unconscious communication in the primary environment while occasioning a reworking of Oedipal configurations. Through vivid narratives of character analysing a range of adult patients, at times requiring a rethinking of the conventional psychoanalytic frame, Jaron offers a fresh perspective on Bollas in arguing for the importance of considering not only the patient's self experience but also the psychoanalyst's.

This important study will be rewarding to beginning and seasoned analysts alike, offering suggestions for using Bollas' work in the consulting room as well as when faced with the demands of civic life today.

Steven Jaron, PhD, is a psychoanalyst working in the 15–20 National Ophthalmology Hospital and in private practice in Paris. Before studying at the Psychoanalytic Society for Research and Training (SPRF), he obtained a doctorate in French and Comparative Literature from Columbia University.

Routledge Introductions to Contemporary Psychoanalysis

Aner Govrin
Series Editor
Tair Caspi
Associate Editor

Books in the Routledge Introductions to Contemporary Psychoanalysis will serve as concise introductions dedicated to influential concepts, theories, leading figures and techniques in psychoanalysis.

The length of each book is fixed at 40,000 words.

The series' books are designed to be easily accessible so as to provide informative answers in various areas of psychoanalytic thought. Each book will provide updated ideas on topics relevant to contemporary psychoanalysis—from the unconscious and dreams, projective identification and eating disorders, through neuropsychoanalysis, colonialism and spiritual-sensitive psychoanalysis. Books will also be dedicated to prominent figures in the field, such as Melanie Klein, Jacques Lacan, Sándor Ferenczi, Otto Kernberg and Michael Eigen.

Not serving solely as an introduction for beginners, the purpose of the series is to offer compendiums of information on particular topics within different psychoanalytic schools. We not only ask authors to review a topic but also address the readers with their own personal views and contribution to the specific chosen field. Books will make intricate ideas comprehensible without compromising their complexity.

We aim to make contemporary psychoanalysis more accessible to both clinicians and the general educated public.

Christopher Bollas: A Contemporary Introduction
Steven Jaron

For more information about this series, please visit: www.routledge.com

Christopher Bollas

A Contemporary Introduction

Steven Jaron

Routledge
Taylor & Francis Group

LONDON AND NEW YORK

Cover image © Michal Heiman, Asylum
1855–2020, The Sleeper (video, psychoanalytic sofa
and Plate 34), exhibition view, Herzliya Museum of
Contemporary Art, 2017

First published 2022
by Routledge
4 Park Square, Milton Park, Abingdon, Oxon OX14 4RN

and by Routledge
605 Third Avenue, New York, NY 10158

Routledge is an imprint of the Taylor & Francis Group, an informa business

British Library Cataloguing-in-Publication Data
A catalogue record for this book is available from the
British Library

Library of Congress Cataloging-in-Publication Data
Names: Jaron, Steven, author.
Title: Christopher Bollas : a contemporary introduction / Steve Jaron.
Description: Abingdon, Oxon ; New York, NY : Routledge, 2022. |
   Includes bibliographical references and index. |
Identifiers: LCCN 2021048131 (print) | LCCN 2021048132 (ebook) |
   ISBN 9780367819552 (hbk) | ISBN 9780367819569 (pbk) |
   ISBN 9781003010999 (ebk)
Subjects: LCSH: Bollas, Christopher. | Psychoanalysts—Biography. |
   Parapsychology.
Classification: LCC BF109.B6435 J37 2022 (print) | LCC BF109.B6435 (ebook) |
   DDC 150.19/5092 [B]—dc23/eng/20211208
LC record available at https://lccn.loc.gov/2021048131
LC ebook record available at https://lccn.loc.gov/2021048132

ISBN: 978-0-367-81955-2 (hbk)
ISBN: 978-0-367-81956-9 (pbk)
ISBN: 978-1-003-01099-9 (ebk)

DOI: 10.4324/9781003010999

Typeset in Times New Roman
by Apex CoVantage, LLC

For B.G. and V. J.-C.

Contents

Preface

The aim of this little book is twofold. The first is to comment on Christopher Bollas's central insight into the human mind, the *unthought known*. Why the unthought known? Since the 1970s, Christopher Bollas has introduced new ways of conceptualising and practicing psychoanalysis at every turn. Key terms include, in addition to the unthought known, the *transformational object* (conceived of as an early object relation which processes those encounters which the infant cannot yet mentalise), the *maternal order* (unspoken rules permeating infantile experience) and the *paternal order* (a related infantile experience made up of unstated or partially stated social laws) and *psychic genera* (the opposite of trauma and a counter to it, psychic genera are produced by the two partners of the analytic dynamic, the *Freudian pair*). Each sheds light on the matter and means of psychoanalysis, and I shall discuss some of them and others in the following pages. Still other subjects, however, among them the psychopathology of the political unconscious (2018a, 2021b), cross-cultural psychology (2013a), his at-times painfully hilarious fiction and theatre (e.g., 2006a, 2006b) and even—despite its tie to our principal question—the unthought known in contemporary art (2018b) could not be satisfactorily developed here. Be this as it may, the unthought known—the opacity of 'unconscious experiencing' (2013b, p. 72) of infantile and early childhood mental states the vestiges of which form the basis for what is known but not yet thought—is what I take as his foundational contribution, the one upon which the others are built. The book's Introduction outlines what is essential in his elaborations on the unconscious while suggesting some of the outer, biographical threads woven into this understanding. Chapter 1 is a reflection on Bollas's formulating of the unthought known, and this is followed by a proposed clinical extension of it.

The second, tied to the first, is to consider aspects of Bollas's metapsychology in relation to how a psychoanalyst may work in the session. Several case vignettes and studies (Chapters 2 through 6) enlarge on what Bollas suggestively calls the analyst's *self experience* as a way of being 'informed from within, so to speak' (1992, p. 6). Self experience is the living, aesthetic experience of being; it is ontology continuously evolving in which the individual senses and perceives consciously and unconsciously in relation to self and other. It may appear aimless or meaningless or, conversely, directed or revelatory. It is a form of autobiographical being but largely exceeds it as in no way may its full complexity ever be accounted for or recounted (it constitutes thereby a possible source of frustration), even if intimations of it may be described and communicated.

As such, I draw from material that some analysts may hold as extra-analytic—for example, the intrapsychic free-associative swell experienced during a violin recital (Chapter 2) or while riding my bicycle (Chapter 6)—as they fall outside the conventional parameters of the analytic frame. For psychoanalysts do not carry out psychic work uniquely in the consulting room; their minds and bodies are not located in this site alone, and Bollas emphasises how the analyst's self experience occurs not only within the session but also outside it. His precedent is Freud's autobiographical material in *The Interpretation of Dreams*, how it was used as part of the free-associative meanderings constitutive of the founder of psychoanalysis's self-analysis. Thus, while the material I elaborate on is mainly derived from my own practice in a variety of clinical situations encountered today in which, as in any psychoanalysis, one unconscious 'articulates' another, a fair amount of non-clinical matter (literary, musical and plastic) also informs these discussions. In all cases, I adopt Bollas's observations and inventiveness as a means, I should like, to psychoanalysing, that is, to how a patient speaks and a psychoanalyst listens. Not only his investigations, certainly, as referring to him and him alone would suggest an artifice. It might be more accurate, then, to say that since he himself configures (sometimes through considered opposition) the thinking of others—primarily, Freud's, but also Winnicott's, Michael Balint's, Bion's, Heimann's and André Green's, among still others—I have likewise tried to bring them to bear on how I work. But I have principally focused on his conceptualisation of psychoanalytic understanding and practice because I feel that it resonates in a way I find especially meaningful. Perhaps others will, too.

I wish to express my gratitude, first and foremost, to Christopher Bollas for the work he has produced as a psychoanalyst and thinker. He has made explicit concepts that I would have at best only intuited through my own practice and has, in this way, improved it. This occurred as far back as the early 2000s when I would go and see the child and adolescent psychoanalyst Simone Daymas to think together about an autistic child I was treating. In addition to offering her acumen and kindness, she suggested I read *The Shadow of the Object: Psychoanalysis of the Unthought Known* (Bollas 1987). At the time, its author was unfamiliar to me. Simone Daymas's enthusiasm for Bollas greatly helped me in my attempts at approaching and (I would like to think) relating to my very troubled young patient. Indeed, the seeds of some of the conceptual developments in Chapter 1, 'A Psychoanalytic Epistemology: The Unthought Known,' were first sown in my mind while dialoguing with Madame Daymas.

Aner Govrin and Tair Caspi initiated this book project and I am grateful to Marilia Aisenstein for supporting my proposal to Routledge. My thanks to Monica Fraenkel-d'Alançon for her incisive comments on much of the book. I have relied on Sarah Nettleton's indispensable overview, *The Metapsychology of Christopher Bollas* (2017), to broaden my understanding of Bollas's thinking. Unless otherwise sourced, the biographical elements found in the Introduction derive from conversations and correspondence with Christopher Bollas.

Attending György Kurtág's 2012 master class at the Cité de la Musique in Paris prompted Chapter 2, 'Idiom, Character and Musical Objects: "Who, if I cried."'

Chapter 3, 'Hysteria: Insufferable Pain,' and Chapter 4, 'Schizophrenia: The Elephant and the Orphan Child,' relate clinical work with patients each presenting two pathologies to which Bollas has devoted book-length studies, *Hysteria* (2000) and *When the Sun Bursts: The Enigma of Schizophrenia* (2015).

Chapter 5, 'Self Experience in a Covidian Dream,' and Chapter 6, 'Psychic Transformations: Air Hunger,' were drafted early in the spring of 2020 as the coronavirus spread quickly and widely. These essays report some of the challenges of practicing as a psychoanalyst at a time when necessity required keeping an analytic mindset even while the conventional setting could not be maintained. Drawing on Bollas's remarks on the viral Real (2021b), each is an account of how collective material reality had affected individual psychic reality and thereby brought something new to working psychoanalytically. The former focuses on the interpretation of a patient's self experience in one of her dreams just as France was going into lockdown in March of that year, while the latter documents my self experience in the Covid-19 unit in the 15–20 National Ophthalmology Hospital with a post-comatose patient. It bears mentioning here that the dear friend to whom I dedicate Chapter 6 died in New York City from complications related to Covid-19 at this time.

The medical practitioners with whom I worked closely during this deeply unsettling period, comrades all, are too numerous to name individually. Among those I wish to single out are Emmanuel Héron, Céline Jamart, Cissy Soares and Jean Varin but again, there are a great many others. Their clinical intelligence and indispensable good humour made the suffering of many livable. Our task could not have been carried out without the constant involvement of the 15–20 Hospital's administration. A discussion group on practicing in Covidian times, brought together by the Psychoanalytic Society for Research and Training (SPRF), lent me much-needed moral support.

I would further like to thank Darrel Samaraweera of Artellus Ltd. Alexis O'Brien and Grace McDonnell at Routledge provided me with clear and efficient help concerning editorial questions. For permission to quote from the poetry of Emily Dickinson, I acknowledge The Belknap Press of Harvard University Press; for T.S. Eliot's, Faber & Faber; and for W.H. Auden's, Curtis Brown Ltd and Penguin Random House.

The patients about whom I write in these pages require a particular acknowledgment, if only for how much I have tried to learn from them. But further, I must state that the therapeutic process that they have undergone is a testimony to their will to try and live for the better. For the sake of confidentiality, their identities have been altered even while my self experience of the clinical encounter remains. In most cases, this work was carried out in French. Unless otherwise noted, all translations from the French, whether a patient's speech or a work quoted, are my own.

My wife and daughter sustained me while writing. As they listened to me talk about how my ideas were developing, they further encouraged me to explore many avenues of thought and for this I wish to thank them both.

January 2022,
Paris and Dinard

Introduction

1. The 'Internal Echo of the Imperfect Sound'

Christopher Bollas is a signal theoretician and practitioner of the arduous discipline of psychoanalysis in our time, demonstrated as the author of numerous books from *The Shadow of the Object: Psychoanalysis of the Unthought Known* (1987) to *Three Characters: Narcissistic, Borderline, Manic Depressive* (2021c). His works, written with a singular verve, testify to a singular subtly. One may hear in these writings what Wordsworth says in the opening pages of *The Prelude* in which is traced the biopsychic growth of the immaterial vessel containing the poet's inner life. The 'voice' is distinct, and it is the poet's 'own'; while further the poet listens for:

> the mind's
> Internal echo of the imperfect sound.
> (Wordsworth 1805, p. 376)

where the 'Internal echo of the imperfect sound' in the context of this discussion implies, I suggest, the opening up of a space within for what seems incomplete, incoherent, unresolved or absent; or, to put it differently, what Bion termed (borrowing Keats's expression) negative capability and which he defined, succinctly, as the 'capacity for doubt, the condition in which doubt can be

DOI: 10.4324/9781003010999-1

entertained' (Bion 1968, p. 70) within the analytic situation. The mental state the analyst assumes while listening, Bollas in turn writes, 'is a form of meditation, a type of concentration, when one suspends critical judgement and the search for meaning so that a part of one's unconscious may be shaped by the other' (2011a, p. 244). In a word, psychoanalytic listening understood as intuitive, unprejudiced reverie.

The unknown, misrecognition and lack, as well as the negative, are intrinsic to the essentially elusive object which draws Christopher Bollas's attention more than any other, the unconscious, his abiding preoccupation. This is perhaps because the unconscious does not readily yield to clear categorisation or complete understanding. It is unmeasurable and untrappable, and so ultimately ungovernable. Be that as it may, Bollas does not shirk from approaching its elusiveness. In fact, the challenge is faced from the very start, as when he brings out the distinction, for example, between the repressed and the received unconscious. '[M]y intention here,' he writes in the introduction to *The Shadow of the Object*, 'is to argue that the unconscious ego differs from the repressed unconscious in that the former refers to an unconscious form and the latter to unconscious contents' (1987, p. 8). 'Unconscious organization,' he writes in the early 2000s in 'Articulations of the Unconscious,' 'is capable of both receiving or repressing ideas. I pay special attention, however, to its receptive function, because this has not been adequately conceptualized' (2007, p. 36). And *The Infinite Question* closes with this reflection: 'The interrogative function of our unconscious constantly works on that knowledge which we bear within ourselves as our unthought known, just as the force of this knowledge inspires intrapsychic curiosity' (2009a, p. 153). Bollas emphasises the unconscious's 'interrogative function,' qualified as 'infinite.' Knowledge acquired is always partial knowledge and its incomplete character, inherent to its structure, inevitably leads to further inquiry. 'We go on writing poems because one poem never gets the whole account right. There is always something missed. At the end of the ritual up comes a goblin,' remarks Ted Hughes (in Fass 1971, p. 15). Like the poet inescapably surprised by the sudden appearance of the goblin, by necessity Bollas pursues deeper knowledge or, perhaps more accurately, he opens himself up to *receiving* this knowledge. 'The receptive unconscious or, to put it differently, unconscious work that is engaged in reception, is the work that Freud describes when he argues that the analyst's unconscious "receives" the analysand's communications' (2009a, p. 14).

In the course of his cardinal accounting of free association, Christopher Bollas discusses 'Two Encyclopaedia Articles' (Freud 1923a), in which Freud describes the cast of mind the patient is to settle into when beginning analysis: 'on the one hand to make a duty of the most complete honesty while on the other not to hold back any idea from communication.' Among the material the patient is asked to disclose is what Freud describes as that which is 'irrelevant to what is being looked for' because, he argues, 'it is uniformly found that precisely those ideas which provoke these . . . reactions are of particular value in discovering the forgotten material' (quoted in 2009b, p. 7–8). In Adam Phillips's words, 'to speak freely'—free of any orientation suggested by the analyst so that, precisely, speech may meander without apparent logic from one subject to the next—'with someone freely listening, is a radical act, at once historically unprecedented and uncanny, and by definition unpredictable' (Phillips 2011, p. viii). Only then may certain communications convey forgotten unconscious material. Together, the 'free associating analysand and the evenly suspended analyst' (2007, p. 13) make up what Bollas has called the *Freudian pair*.

Freud's primal intuition of how a dream signifies unconscious life lies at the heart of Bollas's metapsychology and is the cornerstone of his clinical thinking. As the analysand reports the previous night's dream, a poetics of the session unfolds: the analyst listens not only to the dream-text but also to what comes before and what follows it in the form of free associations, sensitive to the 'chains of ideas' (2009a, p. 20) and 'logic of narrative sequence' (2009a, p. 30) in which it is embedded. Speech is polysemic and connotative, and the words it conveys communicate more than their literal meaning. In my psychoanalytic reading, Wordsworth's 'internal echo of the imperfect sound' encapsulates what is essential in the process, that is, the vastly associative signifying resonances passed unconsciously between the two psyches comprising the Freudian pair over time. As the analysand and analyst 'regress together' (2009a, p. 20) to a prior, perhaps infantile template of being, there might emerge a new way of putting that experience into a form meaningful to the analysand at the present moment of the session. Bollas emphasises that the self in psychoanalysis seeks to know something about him- or herself that was previously not known but, at best, only sensed. What is unknown about the self, he writes, is situated in the id, in an '*it* within us that we cannot put into consciousness' (1995, p. 148; emphasis in the original). The analyst as transformational object plays an essential role in helping what has resisted conscious understanding come into consciousness insofar as his or her interventions, or silences, mobilise the analysand's unconscious into communicating. If the self is to be experienced in a meaningful way for the individual, then it must be related in some way to the unconscious (1995, p. 179).

One's self expresses the unconscious in the form of character—where *character* 'refers to the pattern of being and relating generated by the idiom of each person's self' (2011a, p. 240; see also 1974). Character in and of itself is thus not necessarily pathological; it is how we are and relate without explosive or prolonged mental or somatic disturbance. A *character disorder*, however, is 'a stylized (and predictable) forming of one's being, more akin to caricature than character' (2011a, p. 239). 'Each character disorder forecloses the receptive and disseminative fecundity of personality in a different way' (2021c, p. xii), they reveal in time the patient's *core axioms*. These repetitive pathological forms of being, which may be acute or chronic, make up what is referred to as *characterology* (2000, p. 11).

Christopher Bollas has theorised and analysed diverse character disorders including those termed *normotic* (likened to Joyce McDougall's anti-analysand)—'someone who is abnormally normal,' 'too stable, secure, comfortable and socially extrovert' and 'fundamentally disinterested in subjective life,' and thereby 'inclined to reflect on the thingness of objects, on their material reality, or on "data" that relates to material phenomena' (1987, p. 136)—and *ghostline*—in which the individual 'utilizes the alternative world to conserve the self (and its objects) with little aim of accomplishing an inner thinking of the unthought known as a transition to bringing true self back into negotiation with the actual world' (1989a, p. 104)—in addition to neurotic, hysterical, schizoid, narcissistic, perverse, depressive, manic depressive, borderline and schizophrenic characters (1987, p. 18*f*; 1999, p. 81–83 and p. 116; 2000, p. 7–12 and p. 169–179; 2013b, p. 13–14; 2015a; 2021c). Individuals suffering from character disorders have sometimes experienced a breakdown early in life as young children or perhaps later as adolescents or young adults, which went unacknowledged and untreated and thus led to a *broken self* (2013b, p. 14). In this sense, speaking of a character disorder is less a way of attributing a diagnosis than a means to apprehending patients who have 'simply given up on life' (2013b, p. 14) all the while acknowledging that it is 'an intelligent attempt to solve an existential problem' (2021c, p. xiii). Bollas's broad clinical thinking, anchored in metapsychology, seeks to get behind mental conflicts whose pathological effects in the entangled form of pathognomonic symptoms have risen to the surface and grasp their '*unconscious* meaning' (2013b, p. 15; emphasis in the original)—often enough but not exclusively in relation to early distress experienced in the shadow cast over the individual by the *primary object*, or the early maternal environment which, as he conceives it, is not reducible to the figure of the actual mother but includes aspects of fathering and thus belongs to both the maternal and paternal orders (2000, p. 7–8; 2021c, p. 2, note 2).

Treatment, then, which in cases of nascent breakdown might require modifications to the setting such as additional and extended sessions, sometimes lasting all day—*Catch Them before They Fall* (2013b) addresses this ongoing challenge—is an invitation to the analysand to speak freely, verbalising even that which seems trivial or nonsensical and further to free associate while the analyst listens in a mental state of free-floating attention, letting elements of the analysand's free speaking mingle in his or her own mind. Perhaps an interpretation is offered. Over time what is constitutive of the analysand's *unthought known* emerges, and both partners of the Freudian pair tangle with it to make it increasingly conscious. That it may become conscious, emerging from the cradle of the primary repressed unconscious, is a result of the analytic process. In and of itself it is not a by-product of analysis; a considered understanding of it, however, most certainly is.

2. Turning to Psychoanalysis

We see how, even in the briefest of terms, Christopher Bollas conceives of psychoanalysis as a way of knowing and a treatment for character disorders. In order to study these questions further, we might ask what brought him to psychoanalysis as a profession. The different elements related to his early psychoanalytic thinking and how he became an analyst are, in the main, three: American, British and French.

He recalls the great help a psychotherapy gave him as an undergraduate studying in the 1960s with the intellectual historian of Vienna, Carl Schorske, and Frederick Crews (who had not yet vehemently attacked Freud in the public sphere) at the University of California, Berkeley. Another inducement occurred while he was managing a bookshop in San Francisco after graduation. A book review drew his attention to Harry Guntrip's *Schizoid Phenomena, Object-Relations and the Self* (1968). He had been seeing autistic and schizophrenic children at the East Bay Activity Center in Oakland, California, where it was necessary 'to invent an imaginary universe' in order 'to imagine their internal world' (see further 2015a, p. 1–37)—in particular, the non-verbal autistic children—in which all the work had 'to be entirely unconscious and intuitive.' Imagining their inner worlds was helped through his reading of Melanie Klein, likened to 'reading Edmund Spenser, a rich Renaissance allegory of good and evil—the good breast and the bad breast—out of *The Faerie Queene*. [Klein]

helped me think, *invent* an imaginary universe with the children.'
Close study of Guntrip's collection of essays on schizoid character disorder was followed by an immersion in British psychoanalytic writings from Anna Freud to Klein to Mahler to Winnicott,
whose 'spontaneous gesture' he found particularly intriguing as it
was meaningful with regard to the 'non-verbal communications'
between himself 'and the children, at the somatic level and at the
character level.' Working with these children was elemental but
not yet decisive. The turning point occurred shortly afterwards,
and it required a departure.

In 1969, he left Berkeley for Buffalo, New York, to do graduate
work in English literature, which involved some teaching. Professors there included the department chair, Norman Holland, who
had trained in psychoanalysis in Boston and had written a book on
psychoanalysis and Shakespeare; Murray Schwartz, with whom
Bollas would write one of his earliest essays, on Sylvia Plath and
suicide (Schwartz and Bollas 1976); Stuart Schneiderman, who
taught Blake and would later seek analysis with Lacan in Paris;
and Leslie Fiedler. Michel Foucault and René Girard were visiting
professors. There he also attended a year-long seminar on Marion
Milner's *The Hands of the Living God* (1969). But primary experience, to use Dewey's expression, that which is unadulterated by a
secondary gaze or commentary, was determinative. A course of his
own design titled Madness and Contemporary American Fiction
included *The Wizard of Oz*, 'a kind of schizophrenic text.' A handful of students remained after class and, to his dismay, told him
that they were ill, identifying themselves, perhaps in relationship
to how he had taught the novel, as schizophrenic. What he heard
moved him, as he had already had some experience with deeply
disturbed children. What could be done? He went to the student
health centre and asked the director, an existential psychiatrist, if
he could train as a psychotherapist (2015a, p. 38–54). While at
work on his doctorate, on Herman Melville, he would also see
students as a therapist under the supervision of the centre's director and further receive training in Hartmann's ego psychology at
Smith College, where he would earn a Master of Social Work.

Study with Arnold Modell (on, among other subjects, object relations theory) and Peter Sifneos (who 'would lead the analysand to a Socratic pathway towards the core conflict') in Boston ensued. One psychoanalyst in Buffalo especially impressed him, Heinz Lichtenstein, who had studied with Heidegger before fleeing Germany (Lichtenstein 1977) and whom he viewed as a 'very thoughtful man who didn't speak much' all the while exuding a 'condensed mysticism' (qualities later observed in Bion). In 1971 and 1972, he went to study at the Austen Riggs Center in Stockbridge, Massachusetts, where Erik Erikson was a mentor and, later, friend, Bollas meeting him again in 1985 when he became Director of Education there.

He had also applied to train in the British Psychoanalytic Society (2015a, p. 55–64). Writing to Bollas while he was still in the United States, Enid Balint asked him to be sponsored by two American psychoanalysts before interviewing. The letters were provided by Heinz Lichtenstein and the child psychoanalyst Albert Solnit, the latter of whom had co-authored several books with Anna Freud. Meeting Bollas in London, Enid Balint asked if there was a particular group in which he wished to train—the Kleinians, the Anna Freudians or the Independents (Kohon 1986, p. 24–73; Rayner 1991; Parsons 2014, p. 184–204)—but he was not aware that such groups existed. He was further struck by the unconventional admission process. There was a marked informality among certain analysts, perhaps a ludic means of loosening defences and opening the candidate up. His meeting with Eric Brenman consisted not in talking directly about himself, but in discussing a Shakespeare play of his choice, Brenman's way of assessing Bollas's capacity for playing with paradox and the counterintuitive. Bollas extended the procedure by focusing on the one he found most irritating (sensing Brenman's unconventionality, he himself chose to be unconventional by *not* discussing the play he most preferred): *King Lear*, lines from which would nevertheless later give the title to *The Mystery of Things* (1999, p. vii; he moreover returns to *Lear* on p. 125 in his discussion on André Green's dead mother syndrome and maternal, psychic abandonment). Enid

Balint asked him whom he wished to be analysed by. He might have opted for Brenman. That he was a Kleinian was of little importance to him. But he also knew Marion Milner's and Masud Khan's respective works. Enid Balint arranged to meet them both. He thought Marion Milner resembled Katherine Hepburn, 'absolutely beautiful' and 'spiritual' but 'frail.' While she became a lifelong friend, he sensed that he needed someone 'strong.' Enid Balint suggested that he and Masud Khan 'might make a very good pair,' and the choice was made during the flight back to the United States. For the year that preceded his move to London in September 1973, 'a transitional' period, he and Masud Khan corresponded and once back he undertook a two-year-long training analysis (1989b, p. 336–337; see further 2013a, p. 80–81, 86 and 141 note 18) and began to attend the meetings of the Independent group after his second year as a candidate, as his analyst was a member.

Training was twofold and so especially intensive. While at the Tavistock Clinic studying adult and couple psychotherapy for four years (six Kleinian and Bionian supervisions, working with Herbert Rosenfeld, Martha Harris and John Bowlby), he was simultaneously supervised (by Paula Heimann and Marion Milner) at the Institute of Psychoanalysis of the British Psychoanalytic Society in adult psychoanalysis. Paula Heimann held that the analysand addressed the analyst, without his or her consciously knowing so, from different points of view: 'Who is speaking?' and 'To whom is this person speaking' (Bollas 1987, p. 1). The patient would speak with the voice of another (such as mother or father or child); and further address not the analyst as such but, again, as another (mother or father or child). What was implied beyond literal speech? A first-person voice was unconsciously speaking in the third person to a second person who represented someone absent from the here and now of the analytic situation. Heimann was 'very direct' and 'always interpreting in the transference based on the reconstructions' while 'using metaphors to allow the patient to speak more freely.' She explained that 'the *me*, the *other* that the patient was speaking to was not *me*, the analyst in the room, but *mama-me* or *papa-me* or *brother-me* or *sister-me*, or part of the self.' The analyst could then offer an interpretation such as 'I think that you are upset that I seem to be competing with parts of you for time in this session, just as part of you competes for time with your sisters.' She further impressed on him that 'the patient was in love' with the analyst, which at first he found 'embarrassing' and even 'shocking' as the Americans he had studied with previously had considered such movements as transference-resistance. Heimann rather underscored 'matter of fact interpretation.' 'How do you talk to this analyst when part of you is in love with him?' Or when the analysand was in distress: 'It's very hard to speak about something that's so private but what do you do with this?' (On Heimann and transference, see further Bollas 1989a, p. 43.)

The Independent analysts who left the greatest impression on him used ordinary language. As he saw it, they were idiosyncratic not dogmatic and he came to understand, perhaps echoing Balint's early essay (1932), that they were 'character analysts . . . trying to find a way to think about how one is affected by the other person's character' (Bollas 2011c, p. xix). Their method of interpreting the transference consisted in, 'Don't say anything to your patient to have an effect, that's manipulation; tell them what you think based upon what you believe to be happening, put it simply' and 'with tact and in a mentally digestible way; then keep quiet.' The analyst is not wholly silent but rather *becomes* silent in order to open up a mental space which the analysand fills in with his or her free speaking. There would be no calculation as to what the analyst should say, as for the American ego psychologists, based on the patient's ego strength and capabilities vis-à-vis the id and superego. That transference should be interpreted *con tatto* and not systematically represents a marked difference from that technique practiced by Kleinians, a position likewise shared by André Green (Green 2011, p. 14*f*), and whose practice was early on suggested by Ferenczi (Ferenczi 1928, p. 99*f*; Parsons 2014, p. 188 and 222). Transference interpretations should, in principle, neither fix a meaning nor be forced or restrictive. Meanings are multiple, and the recognition of the vast heterogeneity of unconscious material further requires that interpretations remain open to revision.

He qualified with the British Society in 1977, but a rattling question had to be asked. The then-institutional structure within the British Society, against a backdrop of political and intellectual changes with Winnicott and Michael Balint, both first-generation Independents, having died even before he arrived in London, and Masud Khan having broken down (Bollas 2011c, p. xviii), led him to consider his future. Paula Heimann, Peter Hildebrand and Adam Limentani advised him not to work within the British Psychoanalytical Society. For some, such counsel would be regrettable, even cruel. But it seemed only to confirm Bollas's implacable need to look onwards and advance towards the development of his own psychoanalytic epistemology. Who, then, would Christopher Bollas row for? Oxford or Cambridge? As it happens, the answer was: Neither. Rather, even before beginning training in London, he had boarded the Pequod and there he would stay, remaining, in a manner of speaking, independent even of the Independents, probing the depths in search of indices of the unconscious. But we must further ask, while aboard the Pequod was he sailing with the naïve innocence of Ishmael or the monomaniacal determination of Ahab? Again, the answer is not simple. Perhaps his mindset combined something of both, and this made for a particular creature. While remaining a member of the British Society and practicing privately in Britain during this period (Bollas 2015a, p. 65–73) and later in the United States, he would teach as a visiting professor at the Institute of Child Neuropsychiatry in the University of Rome, lecturing on Winnicott, for instance, and exchange with groups of Scandinavian analysts in Sweden. With Jonathan Sklar, he would also found 'theothergroup' or TOG in London about which, Sklar writes, 'We thought that particular ways of enabling thinking together in a group, utilizing contrapuntal listening to include all ideas without imposing a narrowing theory that can quickly develop into frank prejudice, would be valuable as an analytic listening tool' (Sklar 2011, p. 168). In none did institutional politics impede intellectual pursuit and critical scrutiny, and thereby each provided not only a desirable but also necessary meeting ground (see further Jemstedt 2011, p. xv).

In his overview of the British Independents, André Green significantly described Bollas as 'autonomous' (Green 2002, p. 30). Not only should the word choice not be taken lightly; it was further spoken by one of the two individuals—the second being J.-B. Pontalis—who, Bollas considers, contributed decisively to his growth as a psychoanalyst (Bollas 2015b).

Masud Khan recommended him to Pontalis as a possible contributor to the *Nouvelle Revue de Psychanalyse* or *NRP* (*New Review of Psychoanalysis*), edited by Pontalis and on whose board Khan served as a foreign editor. The *NRP* was becoming a fertile forum for (mainly) French and English analysts having an independent outlook and the two corresponded, Bollas handing him 'The Transformational Object.' Reading the manuscript, Pontalis discerned in Bollas's character something found, he believed, among certain French analysts, that is, a sensibility drawn more to questions explored in the form of searching essays than overly detailed clinical narratives. Perhaps this had to do with Bollas's father's French origins. His first article, drawn from that essay, appeared in the number on the secret, in 1976. Meanwhile, the year before, Pontalis had spoken about him to André Green, who was to give his seminal paper, 'The Analyst, Symbolization and Absence in the Analytic Setting' (Green 1975), at the International Psychoanalytical Association congress in London. The two met that summer at a reception organised by Masud Khan.

On regular trips to Paris, Bollas would lunch with Pontalis and Green (who, like Pontalis, had attended Lacan's seminars in the 1960s before distancing himself from him) on the terrace of the Café de Flore. There in Saint-Germain-des-Prés the three would 'talk psychoanalysis,' comparing and contrasting different ways of thinking and working psychoanalytically. Many British, for example, were excessively clinically oriented (Green, who could be fiercely combative, opposed the empirical use of infant observation, the North Americans' insistence on accumulating and measuring 'data, data!'), while the French were drawn to the history of the problematics of psychoanalytic thinking, what Freud had written and meant and where had he written it. Bollas learned that Green found British Independent strategies of interpretation of interest; not especially Pontalis, who thought of the clinical vignette as 'fiction'—all the while expanding his writing to include fiction. Pontalis spoke about 'what's most interesting in Freud, his contradictions,' and Freud's different models of the unconscious were a case in point. 'He's one of the most honest writers, he doesn't try to clean himself up and he leaves it there.' Despite recognising these unresolvable problems, Freud continued out of the necessity of seeking truth to confront himself with the enigmas arising out of the human mind and how, or if, even, they might be analysed. Retrospectively we may understand this position as a measure of Freud's negative capability, and it is moreover perhaps what Pontalis meant when he told Bollas that psychoanalysis 'was an unrepresentable phenomenon.'

He found Pontalis highly intelligent, witty and refined while at the same time modest and receptive to listening to another's thinking. As a young man, he had studied philosophy with Merleau-Ponty (when he first met Peter Hildebrand) and then Sartre, and he was later analysed by Lacan before parting with him and helping to found the Psychoanalytic Association of France (APF) in 1964. Even before the first issue of the *NRP* appeared in 1970, he had contributed two landmark works: in 1964, *Primal Fantasy, Fantasy of Origins, Origins of Fantasy*, co-authored with Jean Laplanche (its first publication was in Sartre's *Les Temps modernes* [*Modern Times*] in which an essay by Green on Greek tragedy likewise appeared) and in 1967 the *Vocabulary of Psychoanalysis*, also written with Laplanche. Each of the *NRP*'s 50 numbers (the last, on 'Incompletion,' appeared in 1994) began as a theme treated by some of the generation's finest and most original analysts, including André Green, Jean-Claude Lavie, Didier Anzieu and Nathalie Zaltzman, as well as non-analysts such as the filmmaker Claude Lanzmann, the anthropologist Jean Pouillon and the art historian Jean Clair (Gérard Régnier). Older English and English-speaking analysts, especially Winnicott but also Margaret Little, Paula Heimann, Harry Guntrip and W.R. Bion, and American ones such as Harold Searles, whose work was at best little known in France, appeared in its pages. Articles by historical figures were translated and published. Younger analysts such as Laurence Kahn, who would later write a review of the French edition of *Hysteria* (2000) (Kahn 2017), were asked to contribute. Each 'Theme' (*Argument* in French connotes 'reason') to a projected issue, often several pages in length, could be thought of as an essay in and of itself. They were sent out to solicited contributors and were a prick to Bollas's curiosity. Bollas thought that Pontalis's *Arguments* were not only editorial triggers inspiring others to debate the theme and problems to be explored. He further sensed the depth of his psychoanalytic thinking in them and felt in his element when given one (see also Heimann 1980, p. 343 note 1). For the issue on 'The Sexual Thing'—one of Freud's core insights but a notion considered by some psychoanalysts as quaint—from the spring of 1984, Bollas read of the 'primacy of sexuality, of the "representations" and fantasies to which they were necessarily attached' (Pontalis 1984, p. 1). He then sent Pontalis his study of a character disorder he called 'The Trisexual,' in which he writes of:

> that person who 'seduces' members of each sex in order to gain the other's desire of his self. The object of desire is the person's own self, but a self hypercathected as part of an erotic family triangle. [. . . Trisexuality is] a state of desire characterized by identification with and seduction of both sexes in order to appropriate genital sexuality by redirecting it into a threesome's love of one.
>
> (1987, p. 82)

Participating in the *NRP*'s movement and taking from its energy was intellectually invigorating, and Bollas contributed several articles to the journal beginning in 1976, some of which later appeared as parts of *The Shadow of the Object* ('The Trisexual' is one example). In other words, sections of the first book grew out of conversations with Pontalis and Green, were written in English and translated into French where they regularly appeared in the *NRP*, and only in the end found their way into the book. Bollas summarised his gratitude to Pontalis when he described him as one who 'encourages a freedom of thought and expression that is rare in the world of psychoanalytical publications' (1987, p. ix).

With André Green he shared an enthusiasm for theatre and they spoke about Sophocles at length. Why did his plays produce theory after theory? 'The primal scene will always produce new offspring,' Green amusingly offered. In his review of Green's *The Tragic Effect: The Oedipus Complex in Tragedy* (1979) Bollas wrote:

> The theatre is the 'best embodiment of that other scene, the unconscious,' and its representational sensibility lies somewhere between the dream's immersion of the subject in an event and the different means of representation in fantasy where the author's presence is silent and removed from the scene of action.
>
> (1982)

He was further instrumental in disseminating Green's thought among English-speaking readers by having initiated the publication of the French analyst's essay collection, *On Private Madness* (Green 1986), which appeared in the year preceding *The Shadow of the Object*. The lines crossed regularly over the years and André Green managed to finish the preface to the French edition of *The Freudian Moment* just before his death in 2012 (Green 2011).

In addition to theatre and the unconscious, two further shared problems preoccupied Bollas and Green: the analysis of character disorders and what Green described as the work of the negative (Green 1993) in which drive destructiveness was patently operative. On the face of it, these questions were not necessarily related and so could be overlooked. Analysing character disorders was not especially common among French analysts. But Green, a 'polymath' and 'decentred thinker' capable of drawing from

Bion, Winnicott and, despite his many misgivings, Lacan, when relevant, took an interest in it. In order to connect these problems, much had to be debated. For example, they agreed that talking about character disorders in reference to the first topography (conscious, preconscious, unconscious) was not possible but at the same time they were convinced that what was essential in Freud's metapsychology was found in *The Interpretation of Dreams*, even though, at the time (c. 1900), only the first topography was formulated and the structural model (id, ego, superego), conceived in the wake of the Great War, was needed to account for the drives of destruction and death.

The principal concern was to understand how the work of the negative manifested itself in the session. As for the Independents, it was a matter of the analysis of character but often enough in patients presenting pathological psychic structures under the auspices of the drives of destruction and death, particularly but not restricted to the difficult borderline cases that many analysts would not take on. Analysis of a character disorder and the negative inform, for example, 'Loving Hate,' an essay in *The Shadow of the Object*, in which Bollas writes:

> It is my view that in some cases a person hates an object not in order to destroy it, but to do precisely the opposite: to conserve the object. Such hate is fundamentally non-destructive in intent and, although it may have destructive consequences, its aim may be to act out an unconscious form of love. I am inclined to term this 'loving hate,' by which I mean a situation where an individual preserves a relationship by sustaining a passionate negative cathexis of it.
>
> (1987, p. 118)

Loving hate: perhaps a discreet extension of Lacan's portmanteau, *hainamoration* (Lacan 1972–73, p. 84), drawing together the drives of hatred (*haine*) and love (*amour*), Thanatos and Eros in which 'True love spills out onto [*débouche sur*] hatred' (Lacan 1972–73, p. 133). Bollas also needed Green's thinking to advance his analysis of Antonio, 'a self forever forlorn, unforgettable, inconsolable.' Echoing Green on the dead mother complex behind which lies the work of the negative (Green 1980b, p. 167–168), he says: 'The subject's entire structure aims at a fundamental fantasy. . . . [T]o nourish the dead mother, to maintain her perpetually embalmed' (Bollas 1999, p. 118).

3. Swimming Beside the Whale

An array of American, British and French currents, then, combined to contribute to Christopher Bollas's training as a psychoanalyst and to how he first worked as one. A distinctly psychoanalytic consciousness, a form of thinking combining conscious and unconscious processes, is to be found in how they communicate with each other. Yet something, I think, also needs to be said about his childhood. I mentioned earlier that his father was French, but he moved to Argentina and England before coming to the United States. His mother was from California and he was born in Washington, DC, in 1943. As a boy the family moved to Glendora in California and then to other towns before settling in Laguna Beach on the California coast (Jemstedt 2011, p. xiii). While it is true that Bollas alludes to his upbringing throughout his writings, a single sentence stands out as it seems to represent his self experience more than relating how he became a psychoanalyst: 'As an eleven-year-old I was once swimming off the coast, about one hundred metres off shore, when a very small California grey whale—which didn't seem small to me at the time!—passed right by me' (Molino 1995, p. 206). What defining meaning impressed itself on the young Christopher as the encounter with the whale took place and, later, in its *après-coup*? It comes as no surprise to learn that Bollas completed a doctoral thesis on Melville's great novel. He admits, however, that at the time he was unaware of its connection to his boyhood encounter. Soon after he would interrogate the great many facets of the psychoanalytic object, beginning with its function as a transformational process—brought about and maintained for the infant in his or her exchanges with the mother—through his reflections on the reciprocity of *evocative objects* (Bollas 2009b, p. 79–94), notably the links between mother and child and between analyst and analysand, but also how physical objects affect us. It catches the viewer off-guard, just as the analysand's *Einfall*—'falling' (or springing up out of the depths, like Moby-Dick) improbably from his or her mind—interrupts the flow of speech to indicate something that might be unconsciously significant yet not experienced as meaningful. What seems paramount here are the psychic terms by which the child swimmer in the expansive sea grows creatively.

Chapter 1

A Psychoanalytic Epistemology

The Unthought Known

1. Historical and Conceptual Considerations

It is a curious expression. By its seeming instability, the *unthought known* might catch readers by surprise. Some might find it baffling or even willingly provocative. What is *known*? Why, and in what way, is it *unthought*? And what of the conjoining of the two words? Can something be *known* and *unthought* at the same time? Or rather are they in some way opposed to each other? Used together, the words suggest an uncanny quality; they are at once familiar and strange, ordinary and uncommon.

And yet despite the expression's enigmatic appearance, as a feature of the human mind, the unthought known exists as part of the ego's implicit, concealed logic—its unconscious necessities and desires, its inherent, idiosyncratic ways characteristic of being—which come into place in the course of early object relating and the experience of life. A psychoanalytic investigation may reveal its dim vestiges to consciousness. It seems unlikely that an individual would ever become aware of its presence in the mind without the therapeutic method initiated by Freud as a way of bringing unconscious content and processes to light with the aim of helping the patient overcome neurotic symptoms. What does Christopher Bollas mean by the unthought known? This introduction seeks to account for his key metapsychological concept.

DOI: 10.4324/9781003010999-2

A historical investigation is helpful. One finds something of it in and around the time Bollas was writing his first developed psychoanalytic essays in the early and middle 1970s. The coalescing of what is knowable or unknowable and what is thinkable or unthinkable within the psychic apparatus as a distinctly psychoanalytic epistemology is apparent, for instance, in André Green's review of Bion's *Attention and Interpretation A Scientific Approach to Insight in Psycho-Analysis and Groups* (1970):

> Sensualization of objects was implemented through the experiences of realization but the space involved also encompasses any experience of non-realization *which can only be thought*. Bion writes: 'I am thus postulating mental space as a thing in itself that is *unknowable, but that can be represented by thoughts*.'
>
> (Green 1973, p. 117; emphasis added)

Something akin is also found in 'Slouching towards Bethlehem' . . . or Thinking the Unthinkable in Psychoanalysis,' an essay by Nina Coltart, like Bollas, an Independent psychoanalyst, in which she writes:

> each hour with each patient is . . . in its way an act of faith; faith in ourselves, in the process, and faith in the *secret, unknown, unthinkable things in our patients* which, in the space which is the analysis, are slouching towards the time when their hour comes at last.
>
> (Coltart 1985, p. 187, emphasis added; see also Bollas 2021a)

Perhaps a premise of the unthought known comes into the literature even earlier. In a manner of speaking it runs through parts of Marion Milner's *A Life of One's Own* (a pre-psychoanalytic work from 1934 written under the pseudonym, Joanna Field) in which, in the course of her search for the 'facts' of her life, Milner differentiates between 'deliberate' thoughts and 'automatic' thoughts (Milner 1934, p. 51), the former actively sought after while about the latter she asks: 'Might not these apparent beliefs of my automatic self, although I had no notion of their existence, possess the power to influence my feelings and actions?' (Milner 1934, p. 57). While not identical with the unthought known, that which presents itself as a belief arising spontaneously in feelings and actions could well be considered similar to Bollas's concept.

He theorised the conjunction of the unknown or known and what is unthought or thought within the psyche in terms that are entirely his own. This began in *The Shadow of the Object: Psychoanalysis of the Unthought Known*. The subtitle indicates that the unthought known is the book's underlying epistemic principle and yet, while it appears here and there in relation to other notions such as aesthetic experience (1987, p. 32), a living, vital moment experienced beyond its cognitive or moral facets (1978, p. 385), Bollas does not discuss it in depth in any of the essays comprising the volume, as he does, for example, the transformational object (1987, p. 13–29). He establishes the idea in the brief introduction, written *après-coup*, which is thereby at once proscriptive and retroscriptive: the opening pages simultaneously anticipate what is to come and return backwards over that which had been presented even while he goes back to it in the epilogue, 'The Unthought Known: Early Considerations.' Something similar occurs in Bion's *Attention and Interpretation* in which the first of the keywords making up the first part of the title hardly appears in the book while the second is conceived of indirectly. In fact, commenting on this particularity in his review, André Green surmised that:

> the person responsible for the interpretation . . . must do away with the feeling of kinship he might be tempted to establish between himself and the object of his interpretation. To achieve this, he must free himself from his illusory possessions . . . in order to meet with a more open frame of mind what he will be faced with as *intrinsically unknown*.
>
> (Green 1973, p. 115; emphasis added)

In a way similar to Bion's sometimes lapidary reflections on negative capability—the concept is not extensively formulated but rather only suggestively sketched out in the final chapter through his quotation of Keats's December 21, 1817 letter to his brothers, from which Bion derives the psychoanalytic concept—one might consider the formulation of the unthought known as something of an afterthought, as an un- or underdeveloped conclusion. This, however, would be a mistake. Insofar as it is a suspended culmination, it is a highly meaningful one because it opens up the psychoanalytic field onto something that was, till then, unidentified and, as such, unnamed.

Readers readily recognise that the book's title—*The Shadow of the Object*—alludes to a passage from Freud's 'Mourning and Melancholia' which, moreover, Bollas quotes in the exergue. In 1915, Freud was writing of object-loss among the bereft who are unable to undergo a work of mourning in which the object-cathexis gradually weakens, which would make a cathexis in a new object possible. Rather, such individuals are inexorably and painfully locked within the confines of their own loss, and in Freud's portentous words, 'the shadow of the object fell upon the ego, and the latter could henceforth be judged by a special agency, as though it were an object, the forsaken object' (quoted in Bollas 1987, p. xi). The subject's intense and long-lasting cathexis in the lost object, which forms in normal or ordinary circumstances the object of mourning, turns against the individual and punishes or afflicts him or her violently; in such cases, object-loss becomes pathological. This, then, is what Freud means by the object casting its shadow on the ego. But nowhere in his first book does Christopher Bollas discuss melancholia in specifically Freudian terms. Mourning, moreover, only comes into the picture in the case of George, engaged in 'anticipatory mourning' (1987, p. 107) or in his discussion of extractive introjection, which involves a loss of a part of the self through psychic theft (1987, p. 166) and induces a 'paranoid state' of mourning (1987, p. 168). No, he is clearly moving in a different direction from Freud. What he brings to light and describes departs from Freudian insights on object-loss and its effects on the ego. How then does his understanding differ? In essence, Bollas considers how the shadow of the primary object falls on the infant, and in this connection it belongs to the realm of the transformational object. What might be considered a misreading of Freud is, in fact, it is 'a piece of radical mischief.'

At least two earlier developments made this wilful demarcating possible. The first is Bion's theory of proto-thinking about which, Bion writes, 'The mother's capacity for reverie is the receptor organ for the infant's harvest of self-sensation gained by its conscious' (Bion 1962b, p. 158). Here, the infant relates according to the breast's spectrum of primitive qualities, from good to bad, which determines how he or she will develop intrapsychically. The second is Winnicott's reflections on the use of the object: 'the object, if it is to be used, must necessarily be real in the sense of being part of shared reality, not a bundle of projections' (Winnicott 1969, p. 88). For Winnicott, the capacity to use an object is not 'inborn' (his word) but rather the result of the quality of the object within the facilitating environment. This does not contradict his definition of the *true self* as 'the inherited potential which is experiencing a continuity of being, and acquiring in its own way and at its own speed a personal psychic reality and a personal body scheme' (Winnicott 1960, p. 46), a definition Bollas refers to as he builds his own theory of the true self (e.g., 1989a, p. 8) and which moreover has roots in Freud's thoughts on the interrelation of what is innate and what is learned (Freud 1912a, p. 99 note 2). For both Bion and Winnicott, the psychic processes described occur in the life of the infant in relation to the maternal object. In Bollas's terms, early self qualities emerge or do not emerge or only partially emerge while experiencing the transformational object, yet they are nevertheless present as an inherited disposition at birth. Afterwards, if the individual goes into psychoanalysis, the traces of the early object relation will express itself in the transferential–countertransferential *dynamic* (Freud's word, which he uses specifically in speaking of transference, is *Dynamik* [Freud 1912a]; I take it up in reference to the Freudian pair).

Here is an initial statement about the unthought known in relation to the transformational object and, later, the psychoanalytic process:

> The object can cast its shadow without a child being able to process this relation through mental representations or language, as, for example, when a parent uses his child to contain projective identifications. While we do know something of the character of the object which affects us, we may not have *thought* it yet. The work of a clinical psychoanalysis, particularly of object relations in the transference and the countertransference, will partly be preoccupied with the emergence into thought of early memories of being and relating.
>
> (1987, p. 3; emphasis in the original)

Bollas refers to the period before the child attains sufficient language competency, that is, in general, before the age of two, as that during which the unthought known is organised in relation to the transformational object, the primary object. He considers it as a part of the primary repressed unconscious. Memory traces of sensations and events, sometimes traumatic, are retained in a partial or sometimes distorted or disguised form in the primary repressed unconscious and are later expressed in dreams and through screen memories. Or in how the analysand addresses the analyst in the transference, including in the affective qualities of his or her language use (affection, fear, misunderstanding, surprise, hatred and so on) or through exuding a mood (1987, p. 99*f*). Critically, these actual mnemic states cannot be thought of because their inscription in the unconscious is preverbal. In this regard, Sarah Nettleton writes that the unthought known 'refers to the infant's unconscious, learned assumptions about the nature of reality, based fundamentally on experiences that register in the mind before the advent of language' (Nettleton 2017, p. 27).

A different kind of unthought known further exists. Forgotten infantile experiences—unthought yet known memories—from the learning period before the age of approximately five years become part of the received unconscious. The unthought known is the unconscious vehicle by which these experiences are conveyed into adulthood: 'it may permeate a person's being, and is articulated through assumptions about the nature of being and relating' (1987, p. 246). The analysand is not merely scarcely aware of these fundamental assumptions but rather fully unconscious of them, even while these assumptions have become the nescient template upon which his or her life has nevertheless been organised. In brief, they constitute the mind's unwitting, underlying principles of feeling and thinking, of being and relating.

Bollas's most complete definition of the unthought known is not found in the introduction and epilogue to *The Shadow of the Object* but in the next book, *Forces of Destiny*. It is as if he needed to enlarge upon what was not especially developed earlier, all the while acknowledging it as the guiding principle. 'That inherited set of dispositions that constitutes the true self,' he writes:

> is a form of knowledge which has obviously not been thought, even though it is 'there' already at work in the life of the neonate who brings this knowledge with him as he perceives, organises, remembers and uses his object world. I have termed this form of knowledge [in *The Shadow of the Object*] the unthought known to specify, amongst other things, the dispositional knowledge of the true self. More complex than an animal's instinct, which is another manifestation of an unthought knowledge, how much of this knowledge is ever to be employed and brought into the subject's being depends entirely on the nature of this child's experience of the mother and the father. If the mother and the father have a good intuitive sense of their infant, so that their perception of his needs, presentation of objects for his 'use,' and representation of the infant (in the face, body gestures and language) are sensitive to his personality idiom, then he will experience the object world as facilitating. When this happens, we have children who take joy in re-presenting themselves, celebrating the arts of transformation because they have experienced

transformative mothering and fathering and know from the
authority of inner experiencing that latent knowledge can be
given its life.

(1989a, p. 9)

Bollas suggests that what is inherited not only physiologically
but also in terms of idiom is related to what Freud described, in
'The Unconscious' (1915b, p. 180*f*), as the primary repressed
unconscious. The murmuring elements of this inheritance are
'ancestral idioms' and 'infants, at birth, are in possession of a
personality potential that is in part genetically sponsored and that
this true self, over the course of a lifetime, seeks to express and
elaborate this potential through formations in being and relating'
(1989a, p. 10).

In writing of the true self, Bollas is naturally thinking of Winnicott. In some ways, he develops his concept of the unthought
known (those assumptions arising out of the child's upbringing) as
built on a predisposed inheritance (the true self) but in one basic
way he disagrees with Winnicott who, he argues, 'linked the true
self to the id and the ego to the false self' (1989a, p. 10). For Bollas, it is rather the other way around:

If the true self is the idiom of personality, it is . . . the origin of the ego, which is concerned with the processing of
life. . . . [D]rives are always organized by the ego, because
this true self that bears us is a deep structure which initially
processes instincts and objects according to its idiom.

(1989a, p. 10)

The infant's experience of the mother and father and how they
relate to their child will determine whether or not the environment
they provide is good-enough, facilitating.

Perhaps the primary repressed unconscious consists origi-
nally of the inherited potential and then those rules for being
and relating that are negotiated between the child's true self

and the idiom of maternal care. These rules become ego processes and these procedures are not thought through. . . . They are therefore part of the unthought known and join the dispositional knowledge of the true self as essential factors of this form of knowledge.

(1989a, p. 11)

He suggests, then, that the unthought known goes back to 'those experiences in a child's life that were simply beyond comprehension' (1987, p. 246). But what happens to these experiences as the infant grows? The child's psyche holds onto unthought, incomprehensible yet assumed experiences for a long time, waiting for the moment when they become subject to understanding, a mental withholding (or holding within) to which Bollas gives the term, the *conservative process* (1987, p. 246). Perhaps that moment occurs despite the child's, and later on, the adult's, unwillingness or incapacity to reveal it. The child cannot express to others, or even to him- or herself, experiences not only that might be traumatic but also the unthought known itself. It is a paradox that something painful psychically cannot be submitted to the other and must be conserved. And yet, 'There is a wish that some day that which is beyond knowing will eventually be known and then available for forgetting or psychic redistribution (from mood, say, to memory)' (1987, p. 246). That wish is expressed through undergoing psychoanalysis, which implies the desire for changing even that which might very well resist change—perhaps due to anticipating the mental pain many people go through and which may be part of a breakdown. In fact,

The emotional experience that constitutes the release of the unthought known in the therapeutic environment is the fulfilment of an unconscious promise that the child makes to the self. When there is finally somebody there to receive the inexplicably painful, the confusing, the horrifying, most people, who are occupied by deeply disturbing self-states, will break down.

(2013b, p. 73)

2. An Extension of the Unthought Known: The Unknown Thought

Till now I have referred to Bollas's metapsychological concept of the unthought known as a psychoanalytic epistemology which, we have seen, represents the subject's unconscious assumptions originating in early object relations and in particular the transformational object and the primary environment. In fact, it is only part of that epistemology. The true self, the subject's inherited predisposition or idiom, is overshadowed until thought becomes known, that is, until what had been assumed becomes a form of incarnated, living knowledge. It is thus that Bollas also uses the expression, *thought known*, if only very rarely in *The Shadow of the Object*. It appears most prominently in the book's last pages, the epilogue where he writes that the psychoanalytic process 'partly recapitulates ontogenesis' (1987, p. 281), or the beginnings of individual growth. The unthought known is uncovered by the Freudian pair, who transform it in the course of their intersubjective communications into the thought known. In other words, a psychoanalysis summarises the subject's earliest object relating but in a new form, an *interformality*, or a 'reciprocal movement of the idioms of two selves' (2011a, p. 246) mediated through transference and countertransference. The Freudian pair brings the unthought known into consciousness where it becomes an object capable of being discerned: 'The transference-countertransference interaction, then, is an expression of the unthought known' (1987, p. 230). Undertaking a psychoanalysis involves 'the reliving through language of that which is known but not yet thought' (1987, p. 4); in other words, what is called the unthought known.

There are times, for instance, when the analysis is 'wordless,' just as in the baby's beginnings in relation to the mother: two libidinal bodies relate to each other in silence. Here, the suggested parallel is between mothering in infancy and the psychoanalysis: 'The infant-mother dialogue is more an operational and less a representational form of knowledge. And the analyst, like the infant becoming a child, will struggle *to move* the unthought known into the thought known' (1987, p. 281; emphasis in the original). The 'struggle,' in the analytic process, is for the analyst to bring the analysand's unthought known into consciousness, or the thought known. It is evident that the analysand also plays a role, but that role is different: the analysand subjects him- or herself to analysis, speaking freely while the analyst, through interpretation, facilitates the rise of what is unconscious into the conscience. One might additionally hypothesise the existence of mental contents that are wholly opposite from the thought known, what we may call the *unthought unknown*. However, a human being imbued with the unthought unknown would have neither an unconscious nor a conscience. In short, this zombie entity—'zombie' should not be understood in its colloquial sense—would have no mind at all to speak of.

Something more living or vital, however, occurs in the analytic relationship and one might imagine still another term, the *unknown thought*, as designating that aesthetic dimension of the self experience of the countertransference dynamic in which a fleeting feeling or intuition arises related to the analysand. As such, what I am calling an unknown thought exists prior to the thought known. It seems to me that Paula Heimann, in her pivotal essay on countertransference, describes this particular phenomenon without however giving it a name:

> There will be stretches in the analytic work when the analyst who combines free attention with free emotional responses does not register his feelings as a problem, because they are in accord with the meaning he understands. But often the emotions roused in him are much nearer to the heart of the matter than his reasoning, or, to put it in other words, *his unconscious perception of the patient's unconscious is more acute and in advance of his conscious conception of the situation.*
>
> (Heimann 1950, p. 75; emphasis added)

When one unconscious addresses another or, more specifically, when the analyst's unconscious perceives material from the analysand's unconscious prior to attempting to make any verbalised

formulation of it, it is a matter of the unknown thought. It is something like what Bion called wild thoughts, 'these wild ideas and
stray thoughts that I consider to be floating around the place in
search of a thinker' (Bion 1977, p. 34), and it is stirred up specifically within the analyst's nether processes in relation to the
analysand's.

I must be clear that Christopher Bollas himself does not use
the term, unknown thought. This is perhaps because the thought
known is itself hardly delineated. But he does seem to refer to
it when he writes, for example, that the 'most ordinary countertransference state is a not-knowing-yet-experiencing one' (1987,
p. 203). Or further when he speaks, in reference to Bion, of 'the
analyst's responsibility to be without memory or desire' as an
'absence of knowing' (1989a, p. 43). I am thus suggesting that the
analyst's unknown thought (or thoughts) appears as a consequence
of the patient's unthought known the analysis of which gives rise
to the thought known. It completes these two terms.

An unknown thought, then, appears as the expression of the
conscious and unconscious intersubjectivity proper to the Freudian pair. In Bollas's triadic organisation, the analyst's unknown
thought and patient's unthought known are not, strictly speaking, opposites. The former belongs to how the psychoanalyst self
experiences his or her free associations and in particular to the
'unthought-out associations. . . [and] our relation to the unconscious as bearers of a significance that eludes us' (1992, p. 132).
The analyst might wish to express what he or she is sensing to
the analysand 'when the analyst may not as yet know the unconscious meaning' (1987, p. 205). Unknown thoughts are not yet
formulated in words other than those conveying something vague
or impressionistic or, as he might say, they 'have a very different
feel to them from concept-driven interpretations' (2011a, p. 244).
This does not mean that the analyst's unknown thought should
be kept to him- or herself while waiting for a more coherent formulation to come to light. It is sometimes necessary or simply
of interest to submit the unknown thought to the analysand, as a
kind of intermediary thinking aloud or thinking-in-progress, to

see how the analysand understands the intervention and if he or she uses it, immediately or later on, as a stimulus or prompt to elaborating their own thoughts. Bion would say that the infant's beta elements are transformed into alpha elements in the course of maternal reverie.

An unknown thought may emerge within the analyst's psyche out of the analysand's projective identification, that which is received, contained and eventually transformed by the analyst before it is returned in a less toxic, more meaningful form. Insofar as it is a matter of projective identification, it is placed into the analyst's psyche by the analysand. It may, for example, represent either the analysand's aliveness or deadness, or something in between. Thus, the unknown thought is induced through the patient's unconscious communications and, as a derivative of the unconscious, the analyst's unknown thought initially lacks clarity. Due to its uncertainty, if verbalised it might be aesthetically experienced as dead, or hardly alive, or otherwise missing the mark. In other instances, an analysand may need a well-formulated intervention in order to feel the analyst's presence as consolidated because uncertainty is unbearable. Such an intervention would not be of the order of the unknown thought but rather something else, perhaps a veritable interpretation that makes the analysand feel invigorated or understood, that is, psychically alive.

In reality, most unknown thoughts are never communicated to the analysand. The analyst keeps them to him- or herself. They are sensed in the course of experiencing equally suspended or floating or drifting attention, a mental state described as 'evenly hovering attentiveness' (see, for example, 1989a, p. 42). Once thought, or brought into the conscience, they might subsequently be forgotten and never recur. Or perhaps they will. Christopher Bollas might consider them as part of the analyst's contribution to the Freudian pair's psychic genera, emerging in a regressive mental state related to formal (free associative) or topographical (dreaming or reverie) regression: 'the ability to move into the meditative state of evenly hovering attentiveness, to receive and articulate projective identifications, to elaborate the narrative contents through inner free associations, and to follow the analysand's mood in the hour' (1992, p. 97).

Having now described the theory of the unthought known and suggested an extension of it, I may now turn to instances, clinical and sometimes non-clinical, in which I've found myself faced with it.

Chapter 2

Idiom, Character and Musical Objects

'Who, if I Cried'

1. The Aesthetic Experience of Music

Experiencing an artwork prompts 'a kind of gathering of internal objects, developing an inner constellation of feelings, ideas, part images, body positions, somatic registrations, and so forth that nucleate into a sustained inner form,' writes Christopher Bollas in 'Being a Character' (1992, p. 58–59). And he says further: 'I am inhabited, then, by inner structures that can be felt whenever their name is invoked; and in turn, I am also filled with the ghosts of others who have affected me' (1992, p. 59). Music experienced aesthetically, as in psychoanalysis, is not reducible to its cognitive or ethical dimensions.

Often enough, though to varying degrees, others, living and dead, some of whom I could not have known first-hand, have a stirring effect on me. Names invoked bring memories to mind and they impress themselves onto my thoughts. Certain aesthetic experiences, when I listen to music, for example, are especially conducive to communing with those who bore these names. Who do I imagine them to be, or to have been? What do their musical compositions evoke? In listening to music, a sense of the present and past resonates within my mind: a given work possesses a present-time presence but it also serves as a kind of window opening onto a complex history at once material and psychic.

DOI: 10.4324/9781003010999-3

2. The Use of a Musical Object

It is March 2015 and I am attending a violin recital at the Hus Gallery in Paris during which Pablo Schatzman will perform works he's selected before a small group of listeners. There are pieces by Bach, Bartók and Kurtág, with the latter's *Népdalféle (in a Popular Tone)* opening and closing the programme while Bartók's *Sonata for Solo Violin* comprises the imposing piece at its centre. Bach's *Adagio* from the *First Sonata* (BWV 1001) and the *Ciaconna* from the *Second Partita* (BWV 1004) along with Kurtág's *Hommage à J.S.B.*, no less important for figuring around the Bartók, round out the evening. My immediate feeling is that the choice of works and the arrangement themselves constitute an artwork, that they are an expression of a combination of the performer's *idiom*, his inherited disposition whose potential seeks articulation, and his *character*, his singular way of relating to others and being himself through the use of *musical objects*.

Pablo Schatzman is perhaps even seeking consciously to communicate something of his self experience to the listeners. What could this be? *Népdalféle* seems to me furtive, and it further evokes in my mind a flayed surface conveyed by drawn-out, shifting discordant and harmonic double-stops (in Kurtág 1989-)—double-stops that recall those in the *Ciaconna*—linked together by slow ethereal glides like two birds in flight circling around each other, modulating their relative distance by a few feet but remaining near—until they set off on their respective courses. The other pieces—the highly intricate weave permeating the Bartók *Sonata* and Bach's—are like dense inner strata layered one upon another. Here and at this moment—an evening at the gallery—a fragment of Pablo Schatzman's character radiates across several stark historical moments and into an ephemeral present before it plunges back into itself and vanishes from the scene.

Here, then, is Pablo Schatzman alone in the presence of others who are themselves alone in his presence with each party nonetheless relating to the other. In what I understand as a variation of Winnicott's observation that the young child's development of the capacity to be alone depends on the mother's reliability in terms of care (Winnicott 1958, p. 33), the performer and his audience rely on each other in a mutually protective way. Our respective vulnerabilities are reciprocally safeguarded from what might be a disruptive form of despair, that of being hopelessly alone.

An accretion of content is built up throughout the six works played (five in name, true; but six total since *Népdalféle* is played twice). Not only are the works chosen for performance embedded within the other, but they are also intertwined. In my mind's eye, I imagine them as if they are growing into each other like vines in a forest tying themselves together, creating a woven mass that continues to move in ways both subtle and not so subtle. Some of the vines hang and swing, and others climb up the trunks of trees while still others interlock themselves into a dense, chaotic mesh along the forest floor, the trees' conjoined roots reaching down below the earth's surface. I tell myself that such inosculation could be a figure for the mind.

From a musicological perspective, each work absorbs the previous one. A later composition registers an earlier one, creating something entirely new while traces of the past remain. This implies a process of cumulative assimilation in order to engage the present inventively. All of the works Pablo Schatzman has assembled were composed for unaccompanied violin (Kurtág's are also scored for other solo string instruments and string trio, as well as piano). Kurtág's work draws on both his predecessors, just as Bartók draws on Bach. Nor do Bach's pieces appear out of nowhere. Biber's own *Six Pieces for Solo Violin* are a notable precedent, even if they manage to express but a slight complexity in relation to Bach's. Viewed psychoanalytically, a musical tradition comprising personal reference points may be understood as feeding the composer's mind, insofar as they become internalised; in a sense, a breast to the infant's mouth. The feeding process might be a source of anxiety or conflict and possibly expressed as such or, on the contrary, it might provide relief from hunger and be deeply satisfying. It might also conjoin the two, integrating by turns inhibition and release in a syncopated somato-psychic movement. Perhaps it functions as a stepping stone to get across to a farther shore. The internalised artwork is a psychic medium through which self experience is searchingly conveyed.

'The idiom that gives form to any human character,' writes Christopher Bollas, 'is not a latent content of meaning but an aesthetic in personality, seeking not to print out unconscious meaning but to discover objects that conjugate into meaning-laden experience' (1992, p. 64–65). One's idiom seeks objects that may help turn seemingly unsignified experience into something meaningful, or to add greater meaning to experience that is already meaningful. An idiom—what, for Bollas, is 'true' in the 'self' insofar it is inherited from one's parents at birth—becomes consciously experienced and part of one's character. In this sense, it is not only intelligible but also further intelligent. In short, in Bollas's conceptualisation an infant is born with a particular inherited disposition, the true self, whose idiom bears this imprint. This idiom subsequently evolves through object relating into a distinct way of being and relating or, in his way of putting it, character.

Kurtág's oeuvre is conceived as diverse messages to others in which echoes of the past arise out of it. There are homages and memorials, postcards and missives, intuitions and thoughts. The source of his creativity is not only a respectful acknowledgment of the past but also a deliberate use of it in which the present is engaged. He expresses himself according to his singular idiom, which is nevertheless rooted in an interiorised musical past. This is perhaps what Winnicott had in mind when wrote that 'it is not possible to be original except on a basis of tradition' (Winnicott 1971, p. 99) and further that the 'interplay between originality and the acceptance of tradition as the basis for inventiveness seems to me to be just one more example . . . of the interplay between separation and union' (Winnicott 1971, p. 99). The composer is at once separated from tradition and united with it. The artwork as internal object, here, a musical object, inhabits his mind and the performer of these works, to speak nothing of the listener, necessarily senses this. What Christopher Bollas calls *ego memory* when speaking about the dreaming individual is related to this kind of inhabited listening: it is a matter of 'the ego's unconscious re-living of the instinct—a re-living that is re-enacted in the way the ego deals with the wish, a handling of instinct that is typical of the subject's ego style' (1987, p. 79). Kurtág's ego style, as expressed in *Perpetuum mobile* (not part of Schatzman's recital), for example, makes use of a quick succession of arpeggios played as *bariolage* that recall those in the *Ciaconna* (measures 88 through 119 approach but cannot, must not reach the ineffable). The overture, played only on the four open strings, further brings to mind measures two and four of Berg's *Violin Concerto*, those in which the open strings are played *andante*, without *bariolage*. *Hommage à J.S.B.*, on the other hand, played *calmo, scorrevole* and in a singing manner, echoes Bach's more lyrical passages. Bach, then, and not only in the *Ciaconna*, constitutes an internal object that inhabits Kurtág's psyche and allows him to compose in accordance with the singularity of his idiom. The predecessor at once anchors the later composer's vast matrix of ego memory and enables it to grow. The short, condensed pieces (like Webern's) are only deceptively 'small-scale'; rather, they represent an incandescent consciousness composing.

I would not go so far as to say that a composer is unconscious of the internal object's 'force of attraction,' to use J.-B. Pontalis's expression (Pontalis 1990); on the contrary, he or she may in the main be fully aware of it and use it in order to induce a transformative operation first within him- or herself, then within the performer, and afterwards within the listener. The internal object affects these three individuals, each of whom may listen in a dream-like state, though awake; a state of consciousness simultaneously imbued with a heightened awareness of itself while fed by the obscurity of the unconscious. Listening is a means to discovering and knowing parts of the self and the other. Not unlike the psychoanalyst listening to a patient's internal objects expressed in a dream narrative as attention floats evenly, the aesthetic experience of listening to music involves a free-floating attention to internal objects communicated through sound. They appear as in a dream, and so sometimes in a distorted guise.

Here is an illustration of how an internal object expressed in sound, a musical object, is simultaneously maintained as such and transformed into a slightly different object having its own attributes. Bartók alludes to the *Ciaconna* in his *Sonata for Solo Violin* when he indicates that the first movement should be played *tempo di ciaconna*. The time signature is three-fourths, just as the *Ciaconna*'s. But the piece has perhaps more in common with the *Adagio* of the *First Sonata*, which opens the *Six Pieces for Solo Violin*. The very first four notes of Bartók's first movement, a chord, are identical to those of the *Adagio* and may be played with a very similar intensity, although the former key is major while the latter is minor. Further, the last three notes of the *Tempo di ciaconna* movement, also a chord, are nearly identical to those closing the *Adagio* (where the chord is played with four notes, the very ones that open the piece), and also played with just about the same intensity. As such, the final notes of this movement do not reproduce Bach's entirely but only approximately. Like the dreamwork, they condense and displace, disguise and reveal, and dissimulate and uncover at the same time. This particular detail indicates how Bartók allowed himself a degree of compositional freedom all the while unmistakably conjuring Bach. One might say then that Bartók's work intimates more the first movement of Bach's *First Sonata* than the *Ciaconna*. This is an unequivocal sign of his willingness to use the past without repeating it literally. The past is present, but the composer is not weighed down, overwhelmed by it. He is not overcome by the past but inspired by it. As for Kurtág, for Bartók the past becomes a necessary condition enabling the composer to create and express something true within himself.

Musicians, despite what some might think, are notoriously pragmatic individuals who are constantly faced with a great number of performance choices that must be resolved in order to execute a piece with conviction, convincingly. Technical problems are legion. They might base decisions on historical convention, a composer's indication, a teacher's lesson or gut instinct. The letters exchanged between Bartók and Yehudi Menuhin, for whom the *Sonata for Solo Violin* was composed, are but one testimony as to how questions of technique enter into composition and execution, all set upon the backdrop of life evolving: 'I am rather worried about the "playability" of some of the double-stops, etc.,' wrote the composer to the performer from Asheville, North Carolina on April 21, 1944 (Bartók 1947, p. vii), while, suffering from symptoms of leukaemia (a diagnosis from which his doctors kept him in ignorance [see Demény 1971, p. 289]), he strove to complete the work. Confiding to Menuhin in his letter of June 30 of that year, sensing that he was in fact dying, he wrote:

> my health is not as good as it should be, the doctors still tamper with me; they say something is wrong with my spleen, with my blood corpuscles, with this, with that . . . heaven knows what is wrong with me (surely not the doctors). Let us hope for the future.
>
> (Bartók 1947, p. viii)

A given listener can grasp neither the weight of life factors that enter into composition nor the immense range of detail a composer attends to when preparing a piece for performance, and doubtless we are not supposed to be privy to this knowledge. A well-played piece makes undisturbed listening possible. The listener, attuned to the array of acoustic candescence subtly expressed, is absorbed in an aggregation of private thoughts and associations. So much outside oneself remains unthought; so much is left to be known. Perhaps, in the context of listening to a musical performance, this absence, or negative, is how it should be.

As with the composer, so it is with a master performer. So it is with Pablo Schatzman. We can never know what effort he has put into his execution, into the expression of thought and emotion, though we can grasp something of its complexity and even deem it bewildering. As he emerges to begin his self-presentation, he projects an intense inwardness and a grave intelligence which deploys itself as the evening unfolds. They are attributes of his mature character, themselves anchored in an archaic idiom and expressing his true self.

Sei solo, wrote Bach on the title page of his manuscript: 'Six solos.' And it is perhaps no coincidence that the violinist's recital of works he's chosen and arranged consists of six solo pieces; but then, the programme might very well be a matter of unconscious creativity. It seems to me that *Sei solo*, written in Bach's very hand, may also signify: 'You are alone.' One may understand this second meaning as an allusion to the composer's state of bereavement after learning of the unexpected death of his first wife, Maria Barbara (Fabian 2015, p. 224, note 25). In the *Ciaconna*, in particular, we glimpse Bach's bitterness, anger and solitude, the feeling that he is now and forever deprived of his wife's intimate presence. And we apprehend his defiance in the face of death, the need to overcome it and perhaps the unbearable awareness of the impossibility of doing so.

As I recall this conjunction of composition and grief in Bach's life, I cannot help but keep in mind how the musician is expressing this spirit to his listeners. Pablo Schatzman performed six unaccompanied pieces which, when considered in light of Bach's polysemic title, are registered as a private work of mourning outwardly expressed. Suggested by the musician's ego memory, loss and how one possibly faces it set the evening's overall tone. We sense the psychic depth of his character and hear what is inherent and specific to his evolved idiom.

Again my thoughts turn to more material questions, to *how* he is playing. Recourse to a largely physical consideration (in a sense, roughly, to the 'hard problem') might be a mental defence against the massive emotional gravity conveyed by the work of mourning performed. I think about bowing and finger movements, pitch and intonation, posture and breathing. But as I gather myself together, I remind myself that these thoughts are not restricted to a material plane, to matter alone. They involve imaginative, associative creativity that makes it possible for the musician to appropriate a musical object for him- or herself and to use it in order to express self experience. Solutions to technical problems in performance arise in sometimes entirely unexpected ways. Finding a solution is not only a question of trial, error, hesitation and the seemingly endless repetition of coordinated micro psycho-motor gestures and movements involving the entire body. As such, resolving a problem, or creating a solution, goes beyond its technical dimension. In all likelihood it involves a kind of playing that grants the performer a measure of creative freedom in order to explore the piece, to use Winnicott's expression, in a non-purposeful way (Winnicott 1971). When it does, the resolution can be altogether ingenious.

3. A Moment from Amelia's Psychoanalysis

While listening to Pablo Schatzman and trying to imagine the many perplexities he would have had to overcome in order to perform, my mind turns to another gifted violinist, Amelia. Recalling Amelia's psychoanalysis gave me an indication, ever faint, of what this kind of problem-solving creativity amounts to. For some individuals with her range of auditory sensibility and imagination, brilliance is less a gift to be enjoyed and shared than an emotional burden that imposes itself in ways at times imperceptible to others. It is experienced alone and so may be a source of distress. She reminded me of Kurtág himself who, when he'd 'hit the bottom' during the middle 1950s, sought help from the psychologist Marianne Stein (Kurtág 2009, p. 24–25). What was the origin of his difficulties? He'd previously believed that they came from someone or something outside himself. The exchanges with his therapist led him to understand that they originated inside. Kurtág began to take his time and compose by making use of only essential form and content, and by listening to birdsong and playing with matchsticks. What he'd previously felt as massive obstacles stifling his creativity and impeding his progress became less obtrusive. His character had changed, and he was able to move forward.

In the second year of her analysis, Amelia told me how, some ten years earlier as an adolescent, she was studying Bach's first *Sonata for Piano and Harpsichord* (BWV 1014) when she was confronted with what for her was an agonising performance choice, so disturbing that she began to lose sleep and miss meals as she became increasingly fixated on it. Should the first bow stroke of the piece be up or down? While the choice before her presented itself in the simplest of terms, it was tearing her apart. Despite what a musician might be able to learn about an entire piece, how a single note is played is ultimately open to interpretation. In the Bach piece, the first four measures are played slowly and solemnly by the keyboardist at which point the violinist superposes a first note, $f\sharp$, which gradually builds in intensity over a measure and a half. Early eighteenth-century custom, Amelia explained, would have suggested a downward stroke, which would have a more soothing quality as the arm and hand lowers due to the pull of gravity. But for my patient, as she recalled her quandary, an upward stroke would have produced something slightly strident as the bow pushes lightly up against the string. It would have been sacrilegious, in her words, to go against contemporary convention, which she felt she had to remain faithful to. And yet, intuitively, given her frame of mind at the time—she described herself as an adolescent seeking her own means of expression but impinged upon by parents and teachers alike—an upward stroke would have been preferable and even necessary. What, then, to do? Remain faithful to tradition or heed the idiom of her opposing self? Her choices were not many. In fact, there were but three: an upward stroke, a downward stroke, or abandoning the piece altogether in a furious attempt at ridding herself of the conflict.

Amelia recalled her painful mental and physical paralysis, an incapacitating inhibition arousing 'deadness' (her word), when faced with her problem. After she'd described it, she fell silent. I let her silence shape itself out of something inchoate, forming something different, that which is shared by two people accustomed to each other's presence. Such calm, still silence—quiet is perhaps a better word—is not suffused with anxiety but, on the contrary, reassuring. Once we had reached this point of solidity, I asked her if she'd managed to resolve the problem and, if so, how? Her reply was razor-sharp, even as the sound of her trembling voice expressed a residue of the despair she'd felt. It so happened that a friend had given her a copy of Rilke's *Duino Elegies* and she found that the poetry, beginning with the first verses, spoke with a directness till then unknown to her:

> Who, if I cried, would thus hear me from out of the Angels' Order?

(Rilke 1923, p. 7; my translation)

When she first read these lines, Amelia recounted, she was able to decide without any hesitation whatsoever what she would do, how she would play. She was trusting her own subjective response, her independence of mind. She could begin to think through her quandary—an unthought known that placed her confusingly as an infant between conflicting maternal and paternal desire—and let her voice express its character without becoming submerged by it. In doing so, it gave her a feeling of being alive. She was, in a word, coming closer to what Christopher Bollas calls *being a character*, in other words,

> that one is a spirit, that one conveys something in one's being which is barely identifiable as it moves through objects to create personal effects, but which is more deeply graspable when one's spirit moves through the mental life of the other, to leave its trace.

(1992, p. 62)

The psychic meaning and value of objects are further examined in the next two chapters. In the first, Bollas's considerations on regression are discussed in relation to a hysteric analysand's breakdown, her recollection of object-loss as a girl, while the second discusses his conception of object use by a psychotic adult's struggle to recover his sanity through his affection for elephants.

Chapter 3

Hysteria
Insufferable Pain

1. Some Thoughts on Regression

Psychoanalysis recognises various forms of regression. Among them, Freud observed at least three: topographical (found in dream narratives, however, fragmentary, and hallucinations), temporal (in which older psychic formations appear, such as a return to the anal stage in obsessional neurosis) and formal (in which archaic figuration modalities take the place of habitual ones). In his 1914 note to the original edition of *The Interpretation of Dreams*, he suggested that 'these three kinds of regression are, however, one at bottom and occur together as a rule' (Freud 1900, p. 548). I take this to mean that they differ from one another but are not mutually exclusive.

Freud's descriptive distinctions gave way to more therapeutic considerations. By the 1950s, Winnicott had fundamentally changed our understanding of regression when he asked whether the early environment failed the child or rather contributed to creating and maintaining good-enough pregenital conditions which would facilitate growth and maturity into adulthood. Primitive ego defence organisations might require analysis in the case of environmental failure during which the analyst should observe the analysand regress:

> When we speak of regression in psychoanalysis we imply the existence of an ego organization and a threat of chaos. There

DOI: 10.4324/9781003010999-4

is a great deal for study here in the way in which the individual stores up memories and ideas and potentialities. It is as if there is an expectation that favourable conditions may arise justifying regression and offering a new chance for forward development, that which was rendered impossible or difficult by environmental failure.

(Winnicott 1954, p. 291)

Over the course of the treatment, the analysand experiences a particular form of regression qualified as 'to dependence' (Winnicott 1955–56, p. 297) on the analyst who handles it by offering a space in which early traumatic experience is relived and becomes part of the 'healing process.' The analysand's trust in the setting makes dependence possible.

Michael Balint further added to our knowledge when, in *The Basic Fault* (1968), he differentiated between benign and malignant regression, the latter 'aimed,' in Jonathan Sklar's words, 'at gratification of instinctual cravings and ... often to be understood as the patient seeking an external object or action in order to enhance, excite, or escape from their object' (Sklar 2017, p. 16), as opposed to benign regression 'in which the patient expects to use the external world as a way of dealing with their internal difficulties' (Sklar 2017, p. 16).

In *The Shadow of the Object*, Christopher Bollas considered what he termed '*ordinary* regressions to dependence' (emphasis added), which requires two conditions: first, 'when a patient begins to regress in this manner, he or she experiences the analytic setting and process as an invitation to regress' and second, 'the analyst must understand this need and be attuned to the elements of the clinical situation which receive the regressive development' (1987, p. 258).

Echoing Winnicott, Bollas argues that the second condition facilitates the first; without the latter, the analysand's regression will be inhibited. The analyst's understanding and attunement revolve around locating the analysands's 'infant or child element.' A critical technical reflection comes up as the analyst must momentarily 'suspend his interpretation of content or transference' until a later moment (1987, p. 259) when the patient is capable of tolerating it and so not experience it as overly intrusive. Bollas, however, is critical of regression to dependence as practiced by Winnicott since 'promoting a state of deep, primitive dependence on the analyst is injudicious and counterproductive' (2013b, p. 105). In order to counter its possible harmful effects, he emphasises 'the analyst's responsibility to give direct attention to the analysand's ego assets, whether as a character, as a relational being or as a working person' (2013b, p. 106).

He further takes up Balint's distinction between benign and malignant regression and states that 'a generative regression to dependence'—benign regression—'is characterised by the analysand's giving over to the analyst certain important mental functions and managerial duties in order to bring the personality back to its childhood moments of origin and experience' (1987, p. 269). However, the clinical picture may very well become darker or malignant when regression to dependence presents itself as out of the ordinary. In his study on hysteria, Bollas further draws on Balint when he writes:

> A regression is malignant if the patient seeks self devolution in order to coerce an other—in this case the analyst— into unconditional care. The analyst is meant to be there on demand; for as long as needed; and in whatever way the patient determines. *The condition is malignant because there is no unconscious intention of returning the self to independence.* On the contrary, the analysis is regarded as the fulfillment of a promise made by the monsters of the environment to make their bad behavior up to this patient by providing an object that would constitute class-action reparation.
>
> (2000, p. 126; emphasis added)

Furthermore, for the hysteric the talking cure is necessary but insufficient; it must likewise combine with what may be called the *showing cure* (2002, p. 107*f*), which allows the analysand to enact the content of his or her traumata, anxieties and what André Green termed, 'erotic madness' (Green 1980c, p. 223, note 1). The hysteric is invited to free associate but in what does such free association consist in? Not only in associating to what is said but also, further, what is shown.

2. Initial Encounters

Mme H was referred to me by her general practitioner. She explained on the telephone that she was seeking relief from chronic, intense pain felt in different various parts of her body and insisted on seeing me quickly as her appointment in a pain clinic was months away. We met the following week.

The seriousness of her character disorder was patent from the beginning, even if it could only be more fully understood psychoanalytically in the *après-coup* of how the treatment unfolded. She arrived in a state of disarray as I indicated the armchair for her to settle into. She quickly pulled herself together, in appearance at least, and handed me a note from her medical doctor while she told me a little about herself. She was around 30 years old, divorced and had a young daughter who lived with her and towards whom she felt very affectionate, despite the child's frequent hostility towards her mother. Mme H herself was an unemployed nurse and could not see how she could continue to work. She considered dropping out of the workforce altogether despite the need to have an income and at the time of her phone call to me, she was no longer seeking regular work. She felt depressed and had trouble getting out and organising the simplest plan. She was overwhelmed by an incessant to-and-fro of psychic and physical pain and took antidepressants and anxiolytics, as well as an antiepileptic, in hope of getting a good night's rest.

During the first meetings, Mme H related how during the morning she would awake in a state of mental fog due to the medication and remain in the warmth and security of her bed, sometimes for hours, after which she managed to bathe and prepare a simple meal for her and her daughter. She could then go down to do some basic shopping after which she returned home, no more than a two-room living space which she described as in need of repair which, however, she was unable to see to due to a lack of money and know-how. She was incapable of reducing the dosages of her medications herself and felt dependent on them. She had been raised with her siblings by her maternal grandmother and a governess on the family estate while her parents lived in a distant village. Both parents were deceased but she had trouble stating exactly when they had died, though she was sure that her father was relatively young and in a state of advanced alcoholism after his wife had left him, and that her mother had died perhaps ten years before her analysis with me began. She seemed to have mourned her father but in her mind, it seemed to me, her mother remained fully alive, as ravishing as the artist's model she had been in her youth while, in the throes of narcissistic anxiety, Mme H watched helplessly as she perceived her own body progressively bear what she called 'the inevitable signs of aging.' Indeed, she described herself as gaining weight and losing her eyesight while her teeth yellowed and hair thinned out. And yet as I saw her the portrait was hardly accurate, unless it rather represented her mental state.

She also explained something about the pain she was feeling. It was especially intense in the abdomen but at times she felt it in her hips and knees. The extensive medical investigations she had submitted herself to and which were still in progress were inconclusive, though 'surely they'll find something.' Over the years she had tried everything to relieve her pain: consultations with specialists, medication, meditation and relaxation, dance, even psychoanalysis, of which she had had two, one after she had freely travelled the world in her early 20s and another as an adult after she had started to work. Nothing came of these 'disagreeable consultations,' which she nonetheless considered 'necessary' but which left her indifferent, if only on the surface. Notwithstanding, she was ready to try psychoanalysis again since she was familiar with the procedure and 'psychoanalysts meant no harm.' Analysis would get herself out a few times a week, she told me, which could only do her some good, as she tried to gather support for her request. I understood these acts as compulsive repetitions having a masochistic dimension related to a traumatic situation or situations that had yet to be worked through, and further tied to a call for maternal care.

Her initial way of relating to me make it clear that she was suffering from uncontrollable and overwhelming affects of loss and emptiness. Her self was 'broken' and I asked myself what form of treatment I could offer. Anxiety hysteria and phobias prevented her from entering into and maintaining fulfilling, long-lasting relationships, so why should analysis this time around be any different? And what of her physical pain? Freud wrote that feminine masochism is 'based on the primary, erotogenic masochism, on pleasure in pain' (Freud 1924, p. 162). And while he believed that it 'cannot be explained without taking our discussion very far back' (Freud 1924, p. 162), how effective could psychoanalysis be in treating it? I observed however that Mme H was very thoughtful as she contemplated certain unconscious movements I suggested to her, for instance, that the difficulty she had in leaving her bed in the morning seemed related to her wish to return to and perhaps remain on the psychoanalyst's couch. She was what Christopher Bollas would call a *transference addict*, a hysteric who had found 'in the cosy eroticism of psychoanalysis a state suited to hysterical life: as the self lies alongside the erotic other, the absence of physical intimacy is itself continually exciting' (2000, p. 150). I nevertheless believed that psychic genera produced by a Freudian pair might attenuate insufferable pain possibly reaching back to scenes of mourning and childhood traumata repeated in later life, in childbirth, perhaps, and so I accepted her request for analysis.

3. Scenes from 'Planet Pain'

Some two years into our work together, as her daughter was preparing to go abroad to be with her father in his native country, she felt intense anxiety at the prospect of the imminent separation. Without specifying whether she was speaking literally or figuratively, she said that her body was on fire at the thought of her departure. She feared that she would never return to her and instead live faraway with ex-husband. Perhaps she could associate with her fear of irrevocable separation from her child, I asked her. She recalled her parents' departures after their brief visits with the children as she looked through the estate's gates off into the distance and how empty she felt at these times as the cathexis in the external object weakened and then faded while the internal object had to take its place, as if it were being 'forced' on her psyche. Perhaps I should not have been surprised when she said that I was torturing her, but in fact I was. Was her remark literal or figurative? Or both? She was living (as she called her existence) on 'Planet Pain' and felt home nowhere, only imprisoned somewhere. She felt 'demolished' and '*amère*' ('bitter').

'*Amère*?,' I asked.
She was silent.

I told her that I heard something additional in her words, suggesting that she felt as if she were '*sans mère*' ('motherless'). She added that her 'victimhood' began while she was in her mother's uterus: 'I was dead on arrival (*morte dans l'oeuf*),' a figuration of antenatal, dissociative fantasies. My interventions were cruel, she told me. When she said this, I then understood that she was speaking literally. While she was in a state of transferential primary identification, she had assigned me as the sadistic mother.

Mme H arrived ten minutes late to the following session and laid down as usual on the couch, remaining silent for several minutes. 'I'm going to get up and go to the window,' she informed me, explaining that the pain was too great along the back of her legs and she was desperate from the arthritis in her neck. She moved to the window, took hold of the handle with both hands, and said in despair: 'I have to walk on my head to move forward. I'm suffering, I can't go much farther on the path of life. There's no solution.

I've fought so hard. Why am I in this state?' I reminded her that her physical pain and her psychic pain were related, an insight she'd already had. She said that the 'state of the world,' with all the terrorist attacks and ignominious politicians, were much like her inner world.

PATIENT: 'Everything is mixed up together.'

I asked her what was driving her to leave the couch.

PATIENT: 'I feel sad and bitter (*amère*).'

ANALYST: 'You can't lie down on the couch because it's too painful. But you no longer feel that you can rely on me.'

PATIENT: 'The pain is in my body, my skeleton. My head is too heavy to bear. I feel dizzy. I tried to see the ENT, she's not there. My GP is going to retire soon. You've also let me down, why am I still here?'

I suggested to her that she felt that I'd let her down just as her parents had and added, 'Your feeling of imprisonment with me is like when you were a child alone with your siblings and grandmother.'

She felt very sad. 'I need somewhere to rest my head but I feel lost.'

ANALYST: 'You've lost a great deal in your life.'

Christopher Bollas writes that the:

> malignant hysteric seeks a formal regression, a regression in the basic form of the self. . . . The formal change is to absent the self as the recipient of the instincts and move it slightly to the side—from associate to dissociate—as the drive now arrives pure and simple in its disturbing choice of object.
>
> (2000, p. 136)

One of the fixation points of Mme H's formal regression, characterised by an alternating of the object's presence and absence, was to a mental state specific to latency when she looked beyond the gates to try and glimpse her parents' arrival or to certify their departure. But there were others. She remembered, for example, how from time to time she would 'dare to climb a tree in the garden,' normally prohibited by her governess (herself figuring maternal will), to see farther away, or simply to rest: there was a small crook in the tree where she would curl up 'like a hatchling in a nest,' an unconscious fantasy of being contained by her mother. Recalling that she had described herself as *'morte dans l'oeuf,'* I asked her 'if the baby bird wasn't afraid of falling from the tree,' to which she replied: 'Baby birds don't yet know any such danger, they're only hungry!' I sensed that this was the kind of playful reply an inquiring young child would make to an adult's question, and it in fact showed how much she had formally regressed. When she was nestled in the crook of the tree, she said it felt as if she was held securely and that her mind was no longer going to pieces. She might fall asleep there and, in the comfort of narcissistic withdrawal, there was no conflict, no pain. What Jonathan Sklar might understand as the 'fragments' of her 'dissociated mind' were contained therein (Sklar 2017, p. 11). I suggested to her that she felt that she could only grow by transgressing the governess's prohibition, in revolt against the injunction. While she reflected on what I had asked her, I also suggested that the bed she had such difficulty leaving in the morning echoed the tree in the garden. Again she spoke about how painful it was to pull herself together.

Hysterics make physical use of transferential objects found in the analyst's consulting room and Mme H was no different. I understood, for instance, that from the moment she sat in the armchair facing mine during our first meeting (when she pulled herself together), other objects in my office could like serve a performative, transferential purpose. Bollas himself states: 'Analysands create environments within the clinical setting and the living through of a mood is one of the idioms for the establishment of an environment' (1987, p. 102). The window handle in particular had become a prop on the stage of her enacted hysteria. She used this object as an expression of her free association whereas for me

it could be used as an object for interpretation. What did it mean
to her? Surely not one thing but many things. What she could not
say, she enacted according to the unconscious logic of her core
axioms. She grasped the window handle tightly in both hands for
fear of crumbling down to the floor. 'I see how you're struggling
to keep standing,' I would say. Just as the window handle was part
of the analytic setting, so too was the analyst and as I could feel
her hanging on to me for what seemed her dear life, I told her as
much—a point similar to that made by Masud Khan in his analysis
of Mrs X when he wrote:

> When this patient was in pain in the sessions she would be
> totally inert and still, and I could meet it, respond to it, by
> what I can verbalize only as embodied sympathy, through my
> body-attention. In such states I felt this patient needed and
> borrowed my flesh and bone to hang on to.
>
> (Khan 1960, p. 159)

The observation about Mme H's frail body opened onto an
association in which she related an accident her daughter had had
when she was an infant, a fall that had nearly killed her. In fact,
when she rushed to see her, she seemed lifeless. 'I was so emptied
out I didn't know what I felt.' I intervened: 'The deepest possible fear and pain.' She remained silent, as if she were stunned.
Stunned yet relieved, as she began to cry. It then occurred to me
(again, I verbalised this to her) that she grasped the window handle as tightly as she had held her injured baby's head: how she
dreaded losing what was most precious to her. It was further likely
that the handle represented her own head seething with pain. As
part of my unknown thought, I was feeling what she herself felt at
the time but was unable to put it into words.

As this aspect of my countertransference gradually became
clearer to me, I offered interpretations of her different usages of
the window handle. She used it at once physically and mentally,
and this opened up its polysemy and created a matrix of meaning
in which affect could meet up with representation. The various

instances of her pain could then be expressed in words. What allowed for this, I think, was that, from a Bionian vertex, my reveries were maternal as was, from a Winnicottian one, my primary preoccupation; but it is further possible that I was the father cathecting the mother and infant imagos combining the maternal and paternal orders, 'processes associated with and usually conducted by the mother or the father, who assume differing forms of significance for the developing infant and child' (Bollas 1999, p. 38). If so, then Mme H could make use of the modified setting which I as analytic transformational object was offering in order to facilitate the joining of affect and language, insofar as she could regress towards her basic fault constitutive of her unthought known with the ostensible hope of repairing it (Bollas 1987, p. 18).

Her body, by means of the 'hallucinatory function' of her dramatisations (Kahn 2012, p. 77*f*), formed the theatre of fantasised desire by which her psychic pain diminished, albeit not entirely. At such times, she felt she could return to the couch and one day quietly asked if I would allow her to.

ANALYST: 'You've become polite, I see.'
PATIENT: 'Was I ever impolite? I can't recall.'

She nevertheless felt guilty for arriving late or not being able to pay for some of the sessions. After months of standing in front of the window, I sensed repression performing one of its vital functions, that of creating an amnesiac pocket in which traumatic formations could remain secure or, to use Bollas's word, 'conserved,' until the time when they could be analysed without producing further harm. On the other hand, I also sensed, as he writes, that 'there is no unconscious intention of returning the self to independence.'

A screen memory awoke to her consciousness following her return to the couch. In it she recalled a merry-go-round she'd go to as a child, seated on a horse like the other children. A game, during which the operator manipulated a piece of rope attached to a pulley on which another short piece of rope was attached and dangling over the children's heads, was part of the ride. The children had to reach up to grab the rope but the operator would pull it up, thereby making it out of reach. One child, though, would manage to grab the piece of rope and be declared the winner. It was never Mme H, despite her effort to stretch her body high enough to catch it. She was always the loser, she deplored. Even as I felt her sense of shame, I elaborated: 'What was play for the other children was a humiliating ordeal for you.' She told me that she thought 'the so-called game was perverse' and added that she was relieved that it no longer existed: 'Children these days don't know about such terrible things.'

The 'perverse,' 'so-called game' of her childhood, however, remained alive within her. But while her contempt and bitterness were still palpable, the hysterical need to act out the cruelty of the scene had largely subsided and instead made it possible for her to relate the events verbally. She was becoming increasingly integrated, psychically at least, and could better tolerate the possible pain aroused by the verbal associative process, a sign that she was settling into an 'ordinary regression to dependence.' At the same time, moreover, she thought it possible to decrease the doses of her medications, which she did in consultation with her medical doctor.

I asked her if the painful memory of the merry-go-round reminded her of any others.

The association she gave was further related to loss and the body. At seven years of age, her mother had savagely cut the long braid, a much cherished ponytail, from her hair, pinning her onto the bed to do so despite her screamed protest. Long hair was too difficult to care for, the mother said, so 'it had to be done.' I let my attention hover evenly over the link between the rope and the ponytail. It was not difficult to associate on: as an object, the dangling piece of rope to be grasped unconsciously evoked for her the ponytail which, she added, her mother kept in an antique case with glass doors, along with other items she considered precious, in the mother's bedroom. As a child, Mme H fantasised the contents of the case, visible through the glass, as parts of her mother's body, specifically her innards. One day, however, she no longer saw ponytail; it had disappeared from the case. A further loss was added to the first one and she felt enraged with, however, no one to express the rage to. The tone of her voice as she related this memory indicated that she was still angered. Doubtless this was also because the cutting of her braid was but a prelude to sexual trauma inflicted by an older male cousin as she was entering puberty, to violence undergone in her body but which was left unspoken for years. Similar to her mother's sadistic cutting of the ponytail, the rape was experienced as murder but before she would die (in each case), her entire being would be overcome with physical and psychic pain into which was intricated deathly Eros: her mother had acted out of love ('it had to be done') and the rape would deprive her of speech and the possibility of sexual desire. Painful sexuality and loss of life, explains Catherine Chabert, are inextricably bound within the melancholic body (Chabert 2003, p. 63–90). Suffering, suggests Bollas, is 'an extension of the self: the psychic equivalent of the growth of a limb that can grasp and hold on to the other' (2000, p. 148). For Mme H., suffering was her characteristic means of binding with, and of growing into, her mother.

Like the topographical, temporal and formal manifestations of regression described by Freud, malignant regression differs but is not necessarily mutually exclusive from benign hysteria. Mme H mainly displayed moments of both benign and malignant regression throughout her analysis. One could doubtless say that she tested the limits of the setting through the malignant compulsion to complicate her progress by means of her many absences, irregular arrivals and inconsistent payment. On the other hand, she needed to verify that I was always present and could tolerate her own absences, and that she could revolt without fearing rejection. While seeing how far she could go might be understood as an act of infantile or adolescent defiance faced with a parent making a demand that was too difficult to meet, I believe that it had more to do with the early maternal environment the insufficiency of which was experienced as largely violent. As such, testing the limits of the setting was an expression of her unthought known. The clinical setting was the theatre for the patient's many regressions which often led us back to the sources of infantile psychosexuality and its development into hysteria. Regression within the sessions, however, enriched her associations and, as she became increasingly confident in and dependent on the setting, Mme H was led to understand and diffuse, if not give up, her formerly pathological identifications. Specifically, these had to do with maternity: she was determined not to behave towards her own daughter as her mother had towards her and, gathering from what she was able to say about her relationship with her, which retained its own distinctiveness in terms of warm and care, there was no danger of reproducing this earlier pathological relationship. Her daughter would in time surely edge herself out of her mother's shadow, and with her own consent. I suggested to Mme H that this courageous act of defiance towards the terrifying maternal object was her greatest triumph and doubtless contributed to maintaining her sense of reality. I nevertheless wondered if this feat was carried out at the price of impeding her from entering into other meaningful, enduring relationships.

I could feel, as we commonly say, Mme H's mental pain. But this feeling was not merely a question of the analyst's empathy in relation to the patient's hardships. It was something that was registered in my own soma. There were moments during the analysis, for example, when my stomach ached. I was not hungry but felted knotted up. Knowledge obtained in the countertransference, writes Bollas, is not only based on sensing the patient's early object world but also feeling it in the soma: 'some analysands enable us to feel somatically rested and receptive, while others precipitate complex body tensions within us which we endure but to which we may give very little attention' (1987, p. 282). Interpretations may in part find their origins in what Bollas calls *somatic knowledge* (1987, p. 282). 'It is well to bear in mind that often a patient's instinctual drives seek a route to mental representation through the analyst's soma, given that the patient trusts the reliable link between the analyst's soma and psyche' (1989a, p. 45). Whereas there was a continuity between my psyche and soma that could make possible good enough representations of pain, which could then be communicated to my patient, in Mme H this continuity had suffered drastically during her early childhood and adolescence. Mme H transferred this dimension of her unthought known onto my psyche-soma. Through analysing my countertransference dynamic, which initially appeared as the unknown thought (remaining in this form for many months), I was able first to mentalise and then clarify it, and subsequently communicate it through my interventions. This helped Mme H to understand the extent to which her maternal object was destructive to her and further help her not to inflict this destructiveness in her relation with her daughter. Psychic genera, to a point, did counter the pathogenic effects of childhood trauma.

4. A Suspended Ending

Lacan once remarked concerning feminine sexuality: 'images and symbols *for* a woman cannot be isolated from images and symbols *of* a woman' (Lacan 1960, p. 728; emphasis in the original). Mme H's mother had, to say the least, a great deal of difficulty in assuming the maternity of her newborn girl and as her child grew she refused to recognise those aspects of her that defined her evolving femininity. The lack of symbolised maternal recognition was doubtless one of the principal sources of her disturbed psychosexuality and ensuing hysterical anxiety.

Her mother, upon her death some ten years before the beginning of the analysis, was cremated and Mme H placed the urn on a kitchen shelf above the stove. I recalled how she felt that her body was on fire at the prospect of seeing her child leave to see her father. A dream narrative she had recounted during one of our initial meetings also came back to mind: 'A dermatological problem, blotches on my skin. It burns.' Soon after, about a year after beginning analysis, she told me that one day she would return to her childhood home with her daughter and scatter her mother's ashes on the hillside but she was then unable to perform the task and, there in the kitchen, the urn stood for years. An unconscious link between her ponytail, withheld by the sadistic mother in the cabinet during her childhood, and the mother's ashes in the urn, which Mme H in turn safeguarded, had been irrevocably established. It was impossible to dissociate the two in her mind and a phobia organised itself out of the unbridgeable chasm between the representation of what the maternal body had been and what it had become, between the exceptionally beautiful, unattainable mother and a handful of ashes contained in an urn. Unable to decathect the maternal order, mourning had been aborted and in its place remained anxiety hysteria girded by melancholic dread. At bottom, Mme H remained a little girl who wished to keep her ponytail at any price, even at the price of attaining a satisfying relational life as an adult.

If Mme H's analysis were compared to psychic matricide taken up in an *après-coup* provided by the setting and the process evolving within it, then her incapacity to spread the ashes was a sign that the fantasised murder was not entirely accomplished, even as the analysis drew to an end. She had inherited a certain sum of money from her mother which she was drawing on for her basic expenses but which, she said, would soon run out. We decided to decrease the number of sessions, leading to a date when the Freudian pair would separate. But at the end of her last session, as she turned to go she said that when the time was right she would ask for another appointment. This was her way of reassuring herself, and me, that she would not be abandoned, irrevocably separated, as she had been as a child. A suspended ending, then. And so the relational tie remained, melancholically, awaiting a time when the work of mourning could be pursued. Like the window handle she desperately clung to for fear of falling, for fear of disintegrating, perhaps, she was unable to let go of what remained—to use Mme H's word—of her mother's 'incinerated body.'

Chapter 4

Schizophrenia

The Elephant and the Orphan Child

1. Blindness and Psychosis

Psychoanalytic psychotherapy with Lucien, a blind schizophrenic in his 50s, shows the complex relationship between the ego 'ultimately derived from bodily sensations, chiefly from those springing from the surface of the body. . . [and which may be] regarded as a mental projection of the surface of the body' (Freud 1923b, p. 26 note 1 [Freud's note added to the English translation in 1927]) and the psychotic's language use; in other words, in the relationship between sensory experience going back to the beginnings of life and the adult's subsequent breakdown. In both cases, we are dealing with the primacy of speech: how the body expresses itself and how the ego verbalises. And of history: the soma's as well as the psyche's.

Christopher Bollas writes in *When the Sun Bursts*, his study of the psychotherapeutic treatment of autistic and schizophrenic individuals: 'I believe that many schizophrenics return to this early sensorial world, to *somatoform experience and representation*. Before wording or conceptual thinking, somatoforms express the self's nascent experience through the body's lexicon' (2015a, p. 152; emphasis in the original). While assailed by auditory and corporeal hallucinations and paranoid delusions leading to frequent hospitalisations, Lucien tried his utmost to retain a connection to reality as it is commonly experienced. In the course of working with him, I observed how he used what Bollas calls *perceptive*

DOI: 10.4324/9781003010999-5

identification to maintain his hold on his object relations—notably through his affection for elephants. Perceptive identification 'is based on the self's ability to perceive the object as a thing-in-itself' (2007, p. 66), as a specific object possessing its own distinct qualities that are not confused by the subject's projective identifications (see also Nettleton 2017, p. 48). As a transformational object, I asked myself, might I strengthen these perceptive identifications through interpretation all the while trying to curtail the advancing destructiveness of psychotic mechanisms?

2. Initiating the Psychoanalytic Process

Lucien was not always sure that he was altogether, of one piece. While in the shower he could sense himself losing his shape and then disappear down the drain, along with the water running over his body. During one of our first interviews, he calmly told me that shortly before he'd plunged or rather 'planted' a knife into his arm to make sure it was still part of himself and not floating along his side. When he felt the blood running down, he was reassured that it was in fact in place. While listening to him my consciousness drifted to Hécaen's and de Ajuriaguerra's study on body hallucinations (Hécaen and de Ajuriaguerra 1952, p. 288), in which is detailed the schizophrenic's sensation of alterations of corporeal unity. The way the subject 'lives his or her body in relation to the world' (Hécaen and de Ajuriaguerra 1952, p. 292) is of prime interest. I also told myself that Lucien's castration anxiety was of the kind André Green characterised as 'red,' that in which ' "the little thing detached from the body" [*la petite chose détachée du corps*], whether it be penis, faeces or baby . . . is always evoked in the context of a bodily wound associated with a bloody act' (Green 1980c, p. 226 and 1986, p. 145 [translation modified]).

The drive's character was destructive. Lucien was indeed violent, towards himself and others, and he had recently attacked his girlfriend, also with a knife. He insisted on keeping the knife with himself at all times since he never knew when he might have to defend himself from 'members of the Brotherhood.' 'They steal my thoughts. My brain flows liquid.' He once took it out to show a psychiatrist who told him that he wasn't allowed to keep such a weapon. 'Everyone carries one in the States, don't they? You're American, aren't you?' If transference onto the analyst occurred quickly, equally important is that he seemed to be testing material reality, seeking to confirm a piece of external, material truth.

Wounds, narcissistic and bodily, were in abundance, as were successive losses—object-loss and loss of meaning. Lucien told me (also during the initial interviews) how he had been separated from his parents shortly after his birth and then placed in a foster home which soon became violent. He then moved in with another couple but was later adopted by a single woman who changed his given name. Lucien, then, was not his name, which he insisted on keeping as a middle name. It soon turned out that his adoptive mother, too, could not care for him and no longer wished to keep him. He tried to understand why she had wanted to distance herself, but could not. He described her mood swings, which he found incomprehensible. I asked myself if they too had become part and parcel of his unthought known. Did they have something to do with how he would try and learn about his origins? As an adolescent he unsuccessfully sought to locate his biological parents. 'I have their DNA and that's all. I don't come from anywhere.' He felt uprooted and basically rootless, essentially without any paternal order or social law. After his separation from the adoptive mother, he went into further foster care. This environment seems to have been more stable and he went to a school for blind children and then as a young adult began higher education. Throughout this period, he surely suffered from infantile depression lasting into adolescence and after, as one object after another disappeared only to be replaced by other unstable, damaged ones. The little meaning life had for him crumbled. Early signs of psychosis appeared at the onset of puberty. He recalled not being sure was entirely present while at school and he had thrown a fire extinguisher at a teacher. It was also at this time that his sight greatly diminished; another fundamental loss. He was born with a severe congenital eye disorder but near-complete blindness took 12 or 13 years to set in. He also required an abdominal hernia prosthesis. 'I feel a bit like the Man-Machine from Kraftwerk. There's this little thing inside me but I've got to keep it if I don't want to burst [*crever*, "to kick the bucket"].' Loss of the 'little thing' inside could mean death. Keeping it meant living like a cyborg, having something artificial inside. But this was different from the implanted false memories, which had no biological function.

A psychotic breakdown occurred years earlier while he was studying at university. It was at this time that Gandhi, his guide dog, had to be put down, and when he began hearing voices. As dissociated as he could be when speaking about how he was unsure if he was all there, he had strongly cathected Gandhi as well as his current guide dog, Queenie, who sat quietly on the floor beside him as he inhaled an electronic cigarette with seeming desperation in order to attenuate the anxiety-producing effects of nicotine withdrawal (so different from the coddled nursling at the mother's breastfeeding blissfully, I associated), in addition to the cats he lived with and looked after and who constituted a kind of family. The psychiatrists had strongly discouraged him from having a family of his own, despite his wish to have, he said, 'a real family.'

His guide dog functioned as part of his body, his eyes. When Gandhi died, he felt he had lost part of himself and his replacement, Queenie, then became 'my eyes, an extension of my body, my eyes.' Harold Searles once remarked that to a certain extent all schizophrenics suffer from sensory deprivation since unlike non-psychotic subjects the schizophrenic individual 'cannot turn to an inexhaustible and well-integrated inner world of fantasy to provide him with "sensory data" of a sort, and thereby fill the void of his sensory experience' (Searles 1963, p. 631). Lucien had further suffered the loss of his vision, depriving him of all that sight provides the ordinary individual. His psychiatrists believed the death of his first guide dog triggered the psychosis. He didn't think so. 'My life began badly and it's going to end badly, too,' he informed me near the beginning of his treatment. I asked him why, if his life was going to end badly, he bothered coming to see me. He didn't really know but my question made him think about his history and his biological parents. He then told me that he wanted to work with me on 'abandonment, catastrophe.' He felt 'neither good nor bad' with me but 'could trust me,' perhaps because of my 'culture.'

3. Attempts at Holding the Fragmenting Body Together

Lucien's body ego was delusional, broken-up. I mentioned that shortly before he contacted me, he'd planted a knife into his arm to make sure it was still there, sensing it floating beside himself. The blood flowing indicated that it indeed was. In this particular sequence, he immediately spoke afterwards about Queenie and the 'foster family' that had brought her up. Queenie had seen her foster family over the weekend and felt comfortable with them. 'She could reconnect with them,' I suggested. 'Yes,' he said, 'she was very happy about it.' He also spoke about his cats and their importance to him. 'They bring me back to reality. When it's bizarre— bizarre for others, real for me—, when I need a hug, there they are.' They provided a sense of a container or contour painfully missing in his life.

An unconscious matrix of associations (see Bollas 2009a) began to organise itself in my mind and then slowly emerge as unknown thoughts. The associations consisted of his broken-up, delusional body ego, his sense of the detached arm and the happy reunion with Queenie's foster family. The essence of Lucien's suffering stemmed from the accumulated caesurae, discontinuities and breaks he'd experienced in his history and body. At bottom, I sensed, was his own catastrophic experience as an orphan, of being 'detached' from his biological parents and passed from one substitute group to the next, and then his futile quest to find out who his parents were, to attach himself to them anew, all compounded by progressive severe vision loss.

Freud writes: 'the manifestations of the pathogenic process are often overlaid by manifestations of an attempt at a cure or a reconstruction' (Freud 1923c, p. 151). Schizophrenia formed a better-than-nothing solution to his pluri-traumatic history, which lay in pieces scattered throughout his life. He then had to submit to psychiatric treatment, which included heavy doses of medication and regular hospitalisations but also the possibility of participating in different therapeutic groups in a clinic, such as a storytelling circle. And he was especially pleased with the sculpture of an elephant he had made in a pottery workshop. The elephant represented elephants in general and possessed a particularly evocative quality (Bollas 2009b). I asked him why he'd chosen an elephant? 'They're also such gentle, intelligent creatures. They have excellent memories and they always help each other out.' He agreed and even found it amusing when I associated on his own association as the Freudian pair carried out its mutual work, mentioning that elephants have large ears and a nimble trunk. He understood that I was alluding to how blind people often possess particularly acute senses of hearing and memory as ways of compensating for the lack of sight and further adroitly use a cane to discern their immediate physical surroundings. As ill as he was, this exchange could not have occurred with an analysand in the throes of an severe schizophrenic episode. It was neither anything delusional nor projective; rather, it was sound and surely resonated with the non- or pre-psychotic vestiges of his idiom and character.

Bollas observes how *perceptive identification* may function among psychotics, for whom:

> safe knowledge is knowledge about a specific object, usually one that has mechanical properties or is in some way a reliable and neutral phenomenon. It does not function as the receptacle for projective identifications; instead it allows the self to engage in perceptive identification that is not invaded by hallucinatory thinking.

> (2015a, p. 176)

One way of approaching the question of how projective identification operates in the schizophrenic is through analysing the value certain evocative objects have for the patient (Bollas 2009b, p. 79).

Concerning the elephant, Lucien initially revealed a greater capacity for perceptive identification than for projective identification.

He added, however, that he brought the sculpture back home, where he kept it in safety. I soon sensed the presence of projective elements when, in a later session, he told me how he had hidden his soul away in a church to protect it from the harm the Brotherhood could inflict. Unconsciously, the elephant and the goodness it evoked signified Lucien's endangered soul. But the fate of his soul, which would become the principal objective of my work with him, was still available to me insofar as it had been displaced onto the figure of the elephant as an evocative object.

Listening freely to his language use was the means by which I might glean something of his unconscious's workings. Lucien himself showed me how speech could do many things. Like other schizophrenics, he tended to take words literally. A caregiver had to be avoided because her name was Boucher, 'butcher.' The sounds words made triggered connections. 'Words are not things,' a close friend told him. 'I'm lacking the symbolic function, my friend says.' Many practitioners working with schizophrenics observe that their speech is 'concrete,' Bollas reminds us (2015a, p. 130). What's occurring is however subtler. He writes:

> In order to return to the sensorial, schizophrenics go through a process of designification in which they strip language of its signifying function. Observers have noted that they seem to concretize language....
>
> What I think is often missed is the logic of this designification.
>
> The schizophrenic is actually *sensationalizing language, turning its signifying function into a sense-property* so that words are divided up into categories of pleasure or pain. If a word is deemed to be saturated with mental pain it is removed from the lexicon, but if it is a safe word it may be used often, in a seemingly talismanic way. Words become things.
>
> (2015a, p. 165–166; emphasis added)

There was much sensationalising language in Lucien's speech but in fact he did his best to understand words figuratively. He tried his utmost to be conscious of how he needed to keep his language enriched, for example, through feeling and metaphor. I told myself that I could perhaps help keep his language use alive, if only by playing with it together in this intermediary therapeutic space. The play, however, had to be played with tact and discretion and even then I was not always sure if I was doing him more harm than good. If intrusive, such play would further deepen already deep and painful wounds.

During one session, he told me that sometimes memories were missing or, if present, false, 'implanted' by the Brotherhood. Shortly afterwards he said that he did not recall trying 'to plant' the knife in his girlfriend. I suggested a similarity between *implanter* and *planter* and that, perhaps, memories, real, or false, were like a knife. He replied by telling me that he could not understand why, after he tried to cut his girlfriend (aiming, specifically, at her heart), he was hospitalised in a secured unit of the psychiatric hospital. I could sense his anxiety and he touched Queenie gently. 'Queenie,' I said, and added with emphasis: 'I suppose that you see her as *your* Queen.' He let off a half-smile, an expression that suggested that the anxiety was diminishing slightly. I then felt that I could ask him about how he expressed himself in the past. 'It was subtler. These days I don't have any distance.' He associated with his girlfriend. They'd known each other for a few years and at first they weren't in love. They then became lovers but after a few years he ended the relationship. 'She wanted something I couldn't give. She was jealous and thought I was seeing someone else. I'm not like that.' He accepted getting back together but she remained snooping. She began reading text messages on his telephone. There was little or no 'distance' between them, the relationship had become unbearably confused. Voices ordered him to 'plant it, plant it, plant it.'

He learned that a fellow patient with whom he had been hospitalised committed suicide. He knew that she was depressive and that she drank. But he liked this person since she was cultured and had even written a book. He saw how she suffered greatly. Lucien seemed to need or want to express something about the primary affects arising within himself and I so asked him how her death made him feel.

PATIENT: 'I felt empty, a lack, but not sad even though it's sad. I don't feel things like everyone else does. It's here in my body, there aren't emotions.'

ANALYST: 'You feel it in your body?'

PATIENT: 'That's it. Emptiness. Like a piece of the puzzle that's missing. Like when I lost my guide dog. Except then I was sad, I cried. Something's missing in my history. Gandhi helped me get my bearings. I miss him a lot. I gave him my food. I went on a hunger strike when I was hospitalised so that they would stop my treatment. I was bored when I was stuck there. Why was I being persecuted? That's why they pump you full of drugs.'

He did not take well to the strong medication administered to him, which diminished his sense of the outer if not his inner world. 'A man tried to get me into his room, to do sex things. I didn't see it coming.' I felt the extent of his vulnerability due to the loss of his sight but also as a schizophrenic, and I told him so. He asked me about my clinical work with the blind. This open, direct transferential address again reinforced my feeling about his capacity for perceptive as opposed to projective identification: I was his therapist but part of being his therapist meant, for him, that I possessed object specificity, an unequivocal integrity. I believe that Lucien's capacity to use perceptive identification was due to his blindness: since his eyes no longer perceived, the loss was compensated by cathecting as much as possible another sensorial pathway that had more to do with perceiving them other than using the existing functional pathways. He took interest in the other's object integrity. He asked about how I approached the blind, and then he recalled something he had not thought about in years.

PATIENT: 'When I could see, I would look at myself in the mirror for hours. Then I didn't recognise myself. It was before I lost most of my sight. When I was eleven or twelve, my cataracts hardened: my blue eyes were hidden behind something pale, white.'

He had lost that vital part of himself and became a stranger to himself. What had been living in him, even while ill, had died. He was in mourning over the loss of his sight. I associated on some verses by Emily Dickinson, not only for the trope of blindness as a kind of exile they express but also for their lacerated syntax, the discrete units precariously held together by the characteristic use of dashes:

There's Grief of Want—and Grief of Cold—
A sort they call 'Despair'—
There's Banishment from native Eyes—
In sight of Native Air— (Dickinson 1863, p. 553)

Lucien continued: 'I started school early because I could read and write at four. (His considerable intellectual cathexis can be understood as a reaction formation faced with the progressive loss of meaning.) But I wasn't as mature physically or mentally as the other kids and so I left for a year. I was bored, it was a terrible time in my life. Soon after I went to the school for blind kids. Sometimes the voices tell me to hurt myself. I don't feel my body.'

ANALYST: 'Sometimes your body goes absent.'
PATIENT: 'Like swimming in a pool and you can't find the edge.'
ANALYST: 'You're afraid that you're going to drown if you can't find the edge.'

Antoine Nastasi writes of psychotic experience: 'What connects delirium and the body is an oscillation between two extremes: infinity and breaking-up'; on the one hand, the experience of the loss of bodily contours as the 'world is chopped-up' and, on the other, the 'explosive and countless sensations and emotions unconnected to each other' (Nastasi 2016, p. 163). When Lucien expressed himself as such metaphorically ('like swimming in a pool and you can't find the edge') and in particular emphasised the great distress the missing contour aroused, I again understood how valiantly he tried to retain a sense of sanity.

During the following session, he told me that he felt that his body was soft, weak. 'Like liquid, or Playdoh.' He felt that his body had lost its familiar morphology, no forms could be distinguished; and he was hallucinating light and colours, 'yellow and green and blue and red.' He trembled as he spoke.

PATIENT: 'I can't see my body in the mirror. The injection [of antipsychotic medication] makes me feel my body because . . . that hurts. It hurts for two days. I'm afraid of everyone, the crowd, the people who read my thoughts. It makes me get lost. If it happens when I'm in the street, I can't find my way and I get very afraid. Not being able to see. I touch myself but it doesn't help me to sense my body.'

His social phobia and fear of becoming lost outside but also of losing touch with himself, of immediate self-dispossession (the core of his unthought known), was tremendous. He was expressing how uneasy he was and so I decided to keep my interventions very short and direct: 'You feel as if your body doesn't belong to you.'

PATIENT: 'I don't know if it belongs to me.'

When he said that his body might somehow be lost, I sensed that we had to do some searching together instead of letting Lucien associate freely alone in my presence. And yet, in a manner of speaking we were freely associating in tandem—something like a normal-sighted person riding a tandem bicycle with a blind person: I was guiding at the handlebar but he was providing much (but not all) of the movement's energy—a remark I shared with him.

ANALYST: 'You feel as if you don't have any hold over your body.'
PATIENT: 'That's more like it.'

ANALYST: 'Your body is living its own life without you.'
PATIENT: 'There's no tie between feeling my body and the voices.
    It's the voices that persecute me, not my body.'
ANALYST: 'Your mind is slipping from your grasp.'
PATIENT: 'Yes.'

This exchange led Lucien to think about a tattoo on his arm, which he had had done when he was at the school for the blind. His association further led me to sense the unconscious logic of sequence, the deep, unseen riverbed over which his speech flowed. The simple design—an elephant—symbolised his group of friends at school, and they all had identical ones. 'Elephants look after each other and live in groups,' he explained. He added that the pain he felt in his arm while the tattoo was being done made it difficult for him to finish the whole procedure; despite this, he managed to have it done. 'Those friends were like family,' I remarked. 'Is that why you put up with the pain?'

While talking about elephants bound together as a group, we could draw out a relationship between the physical pain felt when he got tattooed and the tremendous psychic pain he felt when he lost his parents and other significant objects. Not unlike Lucien's boyhood experiences of foster families and adoption, the elephant gathering symbolised what Bollas calls a *fifth object*, an extrafamilial, social grouping which 'breaks the hegemony' of the family organisation or *fourth object* (2005, p. 111–112). The fifth object, he says, is structured 'along a psychotic axis' and finding oneself within such a group may very well contribute to a breaking-down of the self or perhaps reinforce the shattering mechanisms already at work in the self's breakdown. On the other hand, it 'may also cure the self of damage that has been inflicted' (2009b, p. 112). For Lucien, the fifth object seemed to have a binding function, more akin to the life drive than the destructive drive, even if experiencing pain was the price to pay for belonging to the group.

Shortly afterwards he called to tell me he could not come to the next session. His anxiety about being assaulted in the street by the Brotherhood was so great that he could no longer go outside and he felt it would be best to go to the hospital. His psychiatrists told him that he was suffering from body dysmorphia and with his agreement, he was to undergo a short series of packs, a warm, wet bodily envelop used to get back the sensation of corporeal unity.

I suggested that we have a session in his room, and he accepted. It was austere, with only a bed, nightstand and chair. He sat on the bed while I sat on the chair. He spoke slowly, beginning the session by wanting to know if I was familiar with the clinic he was being treated in. From one of his psychiatrists, he knew that I had once worked in the very psychiatric association this particular clinic was part of, just as he knew about the ophthalmological hospital I was working in because a friend of his saw my name in one of the directories.

I noticed a small stuffed animal propped up on the nightstand but I couldn't make out what it was. 'What's that?'

PATIENT: 'An elephant. A friend brought it for me.'

My thoughts turned to the elephant sculpture he'd said spoken about a few months earlier, as well as the tattoo.

ANALYST: 'You told me about liking elephants very much, how intelligent and caring they are.'
PATIENT: 'Yes.'

I then brought up a comment he'd made at the time but above all my own thoughts about it, which I had not revealed to him.

ANALYST: 'Do you recall? You once told me that you were certain that I had some paintings hanging on the walls of my office. There's a painting or two but mainly prints.'
PATIENT: 'Yes.'
ANALYST: 'You felt that they were mainly black and white, without too much colour. Your intuition was correct.'
PATIENT: 'Yes.'
ANALYST: 'Now that I see your elephant there on the nightstand, I can tell you about one of the prints. It represents an elephant skull.'

PATIENT (WITH SURPRISE): 'Oh yes?'
ANALYST: 'Yes, the backside of an elephant skull.'
PATIENT (STILL SURPRISED): 'An elephant skull?'
ANALYST: 'Perhaps you can tell me something about what this makes you think of.'
PATIENT: 'An elephant skull. . . . Where is its mind? It's only a skull. The backside of the skull?'

Lucien was silent, perhaps conjuring up in his own mind the image of a skull with its departed mind. He added: 'The elephant makes me think of the child. (*L'éléphant me fait penser à l'enfant.*)'

The two words were near homonyms. He had also taken up use of the *faire causatif* associated with *thinking*, echoing my own spontaneous use.

ANALYST: 'The elephant and the child (*l'éléphant et l'enfant*).'

Repeating the words and emphasising their phonetic similarity prompted him to add a third term.

PATIENT: 'The orphan child (*L'enfant orphélin*).'

This led me to offer an interpretation: 'The orphan child you were.' He nodded his head, as if I had understood him and given him some understanding about himself, and then he said: 'The orphan child I am.'

Silence filled the air for several minutes. I took my eyes off of him and my gaze wandered around the small room. It was painted white; there was only dim light since the shutters were partly closed. The half-light made me think of low vision. I looked at the stuffed animal. I then looked at the closed door. On the back hung a bathrobe. Beside it propped up against the wall was his white cane. I noticed a hole in the wall, which I assumed he'd himself punched. I said to myself: 'Here we are.' Then he broke the silence.

PATIENT: 'The backside of a skull.'
ANALYST: 'Yes.'

PATIENT: 'What about the other sides?'

I waited silently for what he had to say next.

PATIENT: 'I suppose it's always a matter of perspective. Which side you choose to take.'

I was eager to hear more about what he was going to say as I felt, in the dim light and quiet stillness of the hospital room, an uncanny movement stir inside me: the print I had described to him was but one in a series consisting of several others, each depicting a different aspect of an elephant skull's anatomy, sometimes highly fantasised and eroticised. Lucien remained silent and so I repeated his remark as a question: ' "Which side you choose to take"?' This initiated what I sensed was an introspective questioning, a deepening of his inner world opening onto the possibility of greater thought and deeper feeling.

PATIENT: 'I don't know why I'm so ill. Do the voices come from the outside or rather from the inside? Perhaps from my unconscious.'

ANALYST: 'They represent something unbearable to you. They are unbearably painful.'

PATIENT: 'They are unbearably violent. So unlike elephants. Why have I become like the voices? I'm not violent.'

ANALYST: 'It seems to me that you're trying to put the pieces together. I suppose that there are so many that it will take quite some time to do.'

The stuffed animal—an elephant—he kept beside him, just as a young child might do, was associated with his own adult feelings about elephants, which led me to talk about skull print about which Lucien further associated by offering a reflection on multiple perspectives. We had moved from the primitive sensoriality of early childhood experience comprising his unthought known to his immediate, far more complex appreciations. His previously held conviction was that the voices of the Brotherhood's members originated in the outside. Something was perhaps changing in his thinking and restructuring in his psyche. One of what Christopher Bollas calls a patient's *core axioms* (2015a, p. 185, see also 2021, p. xii) appeared to be reconfiguring itself into something more nuanced and which might enable more salutary psychic growth, such as when 'the analysand changes her mental position and her behaviour. . . [and presents] her new point of view as her own' (2015a, p. 185). From that point on, it would perhaps be possible to attend to the question of Lucien's drive destructiveness and the unconscious conflicts organising it.

The appearance of Covid-19 onto the analytic scene has challenged psychoanalysts to rethink the therapeutic process. The final two chapters are instances in which I tried to face these demands while continuing to make use of Christopher Bollas's psychoanalytic epistemology.

Self Experience in a Covidian Dream

1. A Dreamer's Self Experience

Among the essential questions Christopher Bollas has pondered is how the self is experienced. In what ways is someone involved mentally while nursing an infant? What of a group of children absorbed in a round of hopscotch? Or a man propelling himself in a wheelchair while avoiding passers-by? What happens in the minds of a grandfather and his adolescent granddaughter while playing chess? How, then, is the self experienced in relation to the object during these moments? What boundaries are momentarily blurred or even lost, only to be found again upon abandoning, interrupting or completing the activity, while others are maintained?

Bollas seeks to understand a psychic movement at once intrapsychic and intersubjective. An individual's psyche creates and maintains internal mental representations of objects, an inner theatre of the self. This is the realm of the intrapsychic. But the psyche is further engaged intersubjectively with other psyches outside it. The first instance belongs to object relations while the second comes under what Bollas has termed *subject relations*. Subject relations are 'a successional interplay of idiom elements' (1989a, p. 80) and subject relations theory 'attends to the interplay of two human sensibilities, who together create environments unique to their cohabitation' (1989a, p. 80–81). The self is experienced, then, through relating at once in the object world, that is, in the individual's choice of object or in his or her use of and by the object, and

DOI: 10.4324/9781003010999-6

the subject world in which environments are intermediary spaces created between two categorically distinct subjectivities.

Freudian psychoanalysis and the later observations of object relations inform this perspective. But Bollas's contribution has a particular colouring, an expression of his own psychoanalytic character. Specifically, his theory of self experience postulates four stages in which the interplay between self and object may occur. First, the self selects an object to use; next, the object, which has a specific integrity or difference, affects a transformation of the self; then, the self finds him- or herself in an intermediary position (what Winnicott termed the intermediate space or third area) in which self and object, previously differentiated, become indistinguishable; and finally, the self is able to stand outside self experiencing and reflect—a *meta* self experience—on that experience (Bollas 1992, p. 17–19 and 31). Such is what occurred to me while I listened to Pablo Schatzman's violin recital at the Hus Gallery.

This way of self experiencing may likewise occur in the course of a psychoanalysis. In thinking about the psychoanalytic process, we find that the relationship between the analysand and the analyst, what occurs in the transferential–countertransferential dynamic, gives rise to a transformation in the psyches of the two protagonists. Two psyches, each possessing as part of their respective histories a distinct idiom and character, encounter each another in a psychoanalytic setting, understood as a liminal space, which is nevertheless inherently asymmetric: the analysand lays on the couch and relates a dream, and then gives him- or herself over to free associating while the analyst listens freely, picking up on the expressions of the analysand's unconscious which may aggregate into an interpretation. Throughout the aesthetic experience of analysis, the self undergoes change in relation to the other (see Bollas 2011a, p. 246): traces of the experience remain and bear signs of that transformation, a function of the maternal order. There occur further moments of taking consciousness, of becoming aware. At such times, which belong to the paternal order, the analysand seems to step outside the analysis and reflect on what's occurring in it. This reflective movement nonetheless always belongs to the transference. It is part of the analysis itself.

The analytic relationship combines both object relations and subject relations. It is a means to attaining a transformative self experience. How might this occur? Outside the session, one has fallen asleep and dreamt, the unconscious choosing representations, some archaic while others are contemporary, from both the inner and outer worlds for material as the self withdraws into oneiric disengagement and undergoes a transformation in which object relations are confused with the self. Upon waking, the self leaves the dream space and might return to the experience when considering it. Perhaps this occurs over morning coffee but it also happens in the course of the analytic session during which the dream-text undergoes further transformation while being told to the analyst. An analysand who brings a dream narrative to the session is immersed in liminal experiencing. The Freudian pair, Bollas writes, 'extends the dream and communicates with it' (2011b, p. 257). The individual in analysis is then plunged into another form of creativity as the:

> ego now grasps that it has a partner, and we discover another pairing: the one between the ego that offers the matrix of its own creativity in the form of the dream and the analysand who transforms the material into a new form of unconsciously worked-upon meaning.

> (2011b, p. 257)

What Bollas describes as the 'wisdom of the dream' is a derivative of the self as experienced in psychoanalysis. It 'lies in its projection of meaning to the dreamer who, if he or she works with the structure of the dream, can transform it into new forms of creative thought' (2011b, p. 257).

2. Signifying Unreality

> Unreal City,
> Under the brown fog of a winter dawn,
> A crowd flowed over London Bridge, so many,
> I had not thought death had undone so many.
> —T.S. Eliot, 'The Burial of the Dead,'
> *The Waste Land* (Eliot 1922, p. 56–57)

The upheaval wrought by the appearance of Covid-19 in the Fall of 2019 struck the entirety of the Earth's population and drove home the indisputability of humanity's fragile interconnectedness. This caesura in time (Bollas 1987, p. 31)—a pause or interruption, a cutting or hewing—propelled many analysts into a crisis mode of functioning in an attempt to assess the traumatic dimension of a viral Real. In the Lacanian Real 'there yet exists,' in Malcolm Bowie's words, 'a world that falls entirely and irretrievably outside the signifying dimension' (Bowie 1991, p. 94). And yet the Real is but one thread entwined with the Symbolic and Imaginary orders in what Lacan called the Borromean knot (Lacan 1972–73, p. 112*f*). The Borromean knot shows how each thread depends on the others (2007, p. 77); it will fall to pieces if one thread is removed from it. In circumstances of intractable psychosis, the Real may, as Bowie writes, in fact lie beyond signification (it is irretrievably foreclosed) yet in other situations signification does remain a possibility. What Christopher Bollas describes as 'the convergence' of the biological and social Real that creates 'a mentally confusing pathogen' (2021b, p. 4) would need to find signification. Something akin to a psychic movement is found, I think, in *The Waste Land* in which the verse, 'I had not thought death had undone so many,' composed in the aftermath of the Great War, encapsulates this bewildering transition from the Real—what is 'Unreal'—to what could be signified, that is, knowledge thought through. By means of a coming into consciousness of what formerly lay below or beyond it, that which was ineffable, the speaker in the poem (who is not necessarily Eliot) now understands the heretofore 'inarticulate element' (Bollas 1987, p. 235)—perhaps an echo of Eliot's 'raid on the inarticulate' (Eliot 1940, p. 191)—and may figure great loss: widespread grief is henceforth symbolised, however unsteadily, however partially.

How does collective external reality affect the self's inner life? As external reality is shared by the Freudian pair, it necessarily exerts pressure on the psyches of both partners. The self is experienced in relation to the object and undergoes change as external reality tints the psyche. Indeed, in the clinical material that follows we observe how the change in the setting of a psychoanalysis in progress, due to the force of the pandemic, catalysed the lifting of certain repressed content in the analysand that could then be used to make analytic progress. But the analyst was likewise affected and (I will detail) my countertransference expressed how external reality exerted itself on my unconscious.

In what I call prophylactic psychoanalysis, in which the setting has been temporally altered in order to protect the Freudian pair from the possibility of propagating or contracting infection while nevertheless engaged in analyst work (Jaron 2020), conscious and unconscious fantasy through absence and displacement, loss and mourning is not diminished, while the traumatic Real of death and mortality—what Bion called '*the* Unknown' (Bion 1940, p. 11; emphasis in the original); what he would later come to include in O (Bion 1970)—might be worked through or, at least, the contours of what could not be previously signified might be delineated. While the physical object is absent, displaced or fragmented, it has been internalised or is in the process of being internalised and it has a psychic quality in terms of presence and absence that the analyst may assess. This is also true for the transferential–countertransferential dynamic experienced affectively in function of physical distance and the different forms of regression, including the topographical, temporal and formal manifestations as well as regression to dependence. Drive motions continue to find representation through objects, in particular, the analyst as transformational object (Bollas 1987, p. 13–29), or fail to, and dream material expressed through speech is associated on and analysed. Most fundamentally, unconscious work—'a *form* of thinking that is outside consciousness' (Bollas 2009b, p. 129; emphasis in the original; Bollas is drawing on Freud 1915b, p. 194)—continues to deploy itself. Despite, and even due to the changes in the setting, the psychoanalyst's unconscious continues to receive 'the derivatives of the unconscious' (Freud quoted in 2007, p. 37) of the analysand. How might this occur?

3. Experiencing the Self in the Nexus of a Dream

Marceline, a university lecturer in biology in her 30s, consulted because she felt unsure about her career and unsatisfactory love life and, she told me, she 'deeply wanted' to get over the problems.

She had read some Freud at school but she now wanted to see 'how it really worked.' Her request for analysis seemed sincere and after some preliminary interviews in which she demonstrated a readiness for cathecting the setting through freely associating on her dream material, we began to see each other three times weekly. The modifications occurred after three years of work during which she was able to relate the difficulties that brought her to analysis, her neurotic character disorder, to a better comprehension of the maternal and paternal orders, that is, of a detached mother who was more devoted to her professional life than her family and an intrusive, impulsive father.

Proposing Changes to the Setting

As the social and biological effects of the health crisis emerged in the first half of March 2020, I contacted Marceline (along with my other patients) to see how she felt about moving to a remote setting where I would be working from my office by telephone or using a video platform while she would remain at her place in respect of the lockdown measures then being rapidly implemented. We would nevertheless maintain the frequency of the sessions. She thought that the change 'seemed reasonable enough' in order to keep safe and that 'we would see how it would go.' Two days later, we began analysis over the phone—her choice, she explained, as she didn't want me to see her living space—where we had left off the previous week in my office.

First Session

I answered her call at the appointed time. She asked how I was doing. I replied by saying that now we were having the session over the telephone. She felt that it was awkward not seeing me, not being in my office on the couch. It was 'very strange' holding the telephone in her hand and speaking into it. She associated this with phone conversations she had had with a former boyfriend and their long-distance relationship. In the end, he left her for another woman. After a time she got over it but now, talking to me, there was 'something disturbing' about it.

I could hear her lighting cigarettes and smoking throughout the session.

Second Session

During the following session, she began by speaking about the drastic changes in social interaction. Like everyone else, she was working from home. She was part of WhatsApp groups and spoke to family and friends regularly. She only went out to do some grocery shopping or have a prescription filled at the pharmacy. It was difficult to work because she was reading news reports over and over about the spread of the virus and how many deaths it had caused throughout the world. She expressed worry for my health. She wondered how long this was going to last and thought the situation would grow worse. There was talk on the news of imposing a curfew. She then recalled a dream she'd had the previous night:

> It was nighttime, I felt lonely, and I wanted to go out for a drink at a café. Perhaps I would meet someone there and bring him home. But I couldn't. I was confined (*confinée*) due to the curfew (*couvre-feu*).

I let my mind drift around the dream narrative and asked her to associate. She spoke of her anxiety. She had been concerned about the possibility of a curfew. She missed her friends. She didn't have a boyfriend. Three words converged in my thoughts due to the phonetic conjunction of [k] and [f]: *café, confinée*, and *couvre-feu*; after which I said to myself, prompted by the second phoneme, '*auto-da-fé* and then, 'We'll be burning heretics soon.' I then began to associate on the word, *couvre-feu*. The literal meaning of the words composing it, 'cover and 'fire,' intrigued me. I said to myself, 'Nighttime passion has to be smothered, the passionate are heretics who will burn.' I asked myself if doing this kind of (prophylactic) analysis was heretical, at which point my associations faded away.

She continued. She felt angry. But she spoke as if she were making a considered, logical argument.

> All the talk about waging war on the virus is garbage. The war metaphor they talk about is used imprecisely, if only because the enemy is not the virus as such but the social and economic conditions that gave rise to it. The virus is but a vector, the weapon, powerful and, as yet, impervious to counterattack (treatment). Politicians have mistaken the enemy. Ok, we have to get rid of the viral weapon, but we also have to talk about the failures that gave rise to it: the bastard politicians (*ces salauds de politiciens*). But if this were to be so, then they would have to address their own role in the virus's emergence.

I was silent as I let her speech sink into me. There was a lot of it to let sink in. At first, I did not know what to think of it, and so I remained silent. She returned to what she now called to the '*sale couvre-feu*,' the 'dirty curfew.' I replied: '*Sale comme un virus*,' 'Dirty like a virus. Dirty like the "bastard politicians."' '

She in turn fell silent. I was not sure if I should prompt her to speak. It seemed to me, as we were speaking on the telephone, that I should. But if she had been in my consulting room, I would have let the silence between us unfold and pursue its course. I decided on the latter tack.

She told me that she felt that she was 'on fire (*en feu*)' but that her anger had to be 'covered over (*recouverte*)' with logical reasoning, 'pulling apart all the arguments the politicians were making.' She then began to cry but did not know why. At this point, it was the end of the session and I informed her of this. She said that she understood. I told her that I would expect her call the next day.

Third Session

She told me that she feared falling ill and dying alone. She brought up how she had cried during the previous session. She had felt overwhelmed by the speed with which everything was happening and that it was she who 'was paying the price for others' bad decisions.' They were 'hypocrite politicians.' When she used this expression (as she had during the previous session), it occurred to her why she had cried: she felt powerless faced with them. I recalled her dream and suggested that perhaps she had some further thoughts about it. Among her associations, she related the *couvre-feu* to how her anger at the politicians had to be *recouverte*: she felt as if she were 'on fire' but had 'to cover it over.' Perhaps, I told her, she was trying to extinguish the fire within because she sensed that it was dangerous, that she could be burnt. I then added that she was telling me how angry she was with *me*, perhaps in the same way she had felt with regard to her mother who was emotionally distant from her and her impulsive, intrusive father but that she was not able to tell them how hurt she felt at the time. She at first refused the interpretation. No, she didn't think that this could be true, but then again, she thought, it might be possible.

She then spoke about our new setting. She was sure that she would go on with analysis, even though she could not come to my office. She felt that it was a necessity and that 'something good would come of it,' though she didn't know what that could be. I told her that making her own decision to continue seemed to do her some good as she had placed herself in an active position, whereas shortly before she had felt helpless.

It was then that I was reminded of her evocation of her long-distance relationship during the first session. I suggested to her that perhaps she felt that in some way talking to me was like having a long-distance relationship. She responded to my interpretation by her silence. I knew Marceline to be quite thoughtful at times and so considered this silence as part of her private mentation which I would respect as the session came to an end.

Discussion

Marceline's psychoanalysis was put into question by external reality, which made it impossible to see her in the consulting room as usual. It was thus a question of how to maintain her analytic sessions. I proposed several auditory or visual alternatives. Marceline preferred to continue by telephone since she did not want me to see her living space but only hear her voice. She thus wished to have a modicum of control over what kind of sensoriality would appear: the visual dimension, anything related to the scopic drive, would be eliminated. Her *substantive self*, 'a content that we transmit to others,' would be conveyed by means of a *transmissive object*, the telephone (2018, p. 51–52; Bollas's discussion of these terms is found in the context of social networks; my use of them differs, as they specifically concern psychoanalytic practice). I would not see her, in particular, when she came to her session and left it or while she was lying down on the couch in my office. Thus, a different representation of her private self was communicated: I could, however, hear her lighting matches and smoking cigarettes in what I understood was a repetitive manner, whereas she never smoked in my office, all the while speaking from time to time about the harmful effects of smoking and the need to quit. In her own way, by smoking during the session itself she was emphasising how the setting had changed. But smoking was further an enactment, an acting-in outside my office that I might interpret later in the analysis in function of her destructive drives. This particular form of enactment, an *outside acting-in*, was related to the virus: smoking was harmful to her health but she nevertheless did so and even flaunted it like a spontaneous gesture during the first session, whereas the rationale for all the changes we had put into place was to protect each other from potential harm.

The first session thus appeared largely factual in content, referring to the specific changes in the setting. It is clear, however, that Marceline's drive motions and affect revealed something latent. There was 'something disturbing' about the changes. There were two reasons we were not seeing each other: the first was the government measures concerning lockdown and the second was her decision not to use a visual platform but only an auditory one (the telephone) to pursue the analysis. She quickly made a significant association regarding our use of the telephone: it seemed to her as if she were talking to a former boyfriend with whom she had had a long-distance relationship. In the end, he left her for another woman. She was distraught and had trouble being fully present at work during the months she gradually decathected that relationship, or at least thought she had.

Marceline felt uncomfortable talking to me on the telephone. This transferential affect revealed material that had been largely absent from her analysis till then, as she had only alluded to it previously: in this instance, through primary identification, I was the former boyfriend who had left her for another woman and, all the while, the fantasised current one (in reality she did not then have one) in the here and now. In other words, we were having a long-distance relationship part of which involved sexual longing. The 'something disturbing' led me to sense that what had happened between her and her former boyfriend was related to why she had asked me at the very beginning of the session how I was doing: not only did the question have to do with my health as the virus spread but it also was something she would ask her boyfriend while they spoke on the telephone. Further, when I thought back to the session afterwards, I recalled a detail I had not given any importance to but which now stood out: she seemed to snigger as she asked how I was. During the actual session, I had no conscious thought as to Marceline's past or future with me or outside analysis, what Bollas describes as an 'absence of knowing' achieved while in a state of 'evenly hovering attentiveness' (1989a, p. 43). My reverie was unprejudiced. With hindsight, however, I understood that in fact the unconscious link between her former boyfriend and me had emerged onto the analytic scene at the very moment the setting had changed and thus in the context of the newly undertaken prophylactic psychoanalysis. While the merging between her disappointing relationship with her boyfriend and that which was unfolding with her analyst occurred to me at the time she spoke about 'something disturbing,' I did not interpret this to her because my intuitions were too vague and hardly formulated to myself. They were part of an unknown thought, and so I kept silent about them with the idea that perhaps later I would evoke them in relation to the appearance of further material.

She expressed her anxiety about the changes in society that were rapidly occurring as the second session began. She tried to defend herself against this anxiety by recalling the ties she was keeping with others (including me) through various social media or by telephone. But she was anxious about going outside and restricted herself to what was essential. Another indication of her anxiety was consulting the news compulsively, which further revealed nascent traumatic potential: she was doing what she could in order to keep herself together but feared that she could very well break down. While I did not understand this at the time that the session was occurring but only in the *après-coup* of my later reflections on it, Marceline was expressing her worry about her former boyfriend living in another part of the country, which led her in an overtly transferential motion to ask about my health. She further needed to know about the duration of the crisis: I understood this as her need to know how long we would not see each other in my office.

A particular worry concerned the possibility of establishing a curfew (*couvre-feu*), which, at the time, was not then in place. This diurnal anxiety expressed itself in a dream that very night in the form of censored desire. The nexus of the curfew dream psychically figured the conjuncture of external reality and psychic reality, and the continuity between these two realities—in particular, with regard to the virus's extensive social and psychological impacts—was patent in the clinical material throughout the three sessions (and afterwards). She had dreamt after the session in which she was smoking and lighting cigarettes. Again with hindsight, it occurred to me that a French expression for asking to light one's cigarette is *Avez-vous du feu?* ('Can I have a light?'). She did not use this expression during the session but perhaps it was implied by her outside acting-in (smoking during the session). Not only was smoking an act of defiance against those who would speak of its danger; it further placed me in an impossible position because I could not give her a light. Still another association I had, again with hindsight, is that smoking could damage the smoker's lungs. Marceline well knew the effects of Covid-19 on the infected person's respiratory system. In a sense, lungs could be set afire

by the virus. (This very psychic configuration burst onto the analytic scene with another patient, Pierre-Maxime, which I relate in
Chapter 6.) As I analysed my unknown thoughts, I recalled something more. Marceline had had a session on the very evening that
Notre Dame Cathedral was ravaged by fire just about one year
earlier. In reality, the fire had started shortly before her session
began and, even with the windows of my office closed, we both
smelt the smoke billowing from it. As she lay on the couch during this particular session, she spoke about how distraught she
was while the cathedral was burning. During the first session of
prophylactic psychoanalysis, I believe that her unconscious was
establishing a link between the fire in Notre Dame, the potential
harm of smoking to the lungs and her disarray about the lungs of
individuals infected with Covid-19. All of this was held tightly
by repression when it expressed itself the night before the second
session in the form of a dream about the curfew. Paradoxically, the
psychic effects of lockdown served as a meaning of easing repression, at which point unconscious content could then find expression through dreamwork.

It is important to note the possibility that I missed some of what
Marceline said after she told me the dream narrative because my
countertransference dynamic led me to associate freely. Marceline's dream-text deeply affected me and inspired fantasies of
heresy with regard to how I was working with her. I was just as
psychically frail as her and became unsettled. Like anyone else in
the viral environment, I was subject to its mentally disorganising
effects and regularly experienced death anxiety (Jaron 2021). Its
countertransferential effects aroused in me a feeling of stupefac-
tion, which led to a number of associations and fantasies related
to repressed sexual desire and punishment for heresy based on
the sound pattern across *café*, *confinée* and *couvre-feu*, with the
[f] inducing in me the expression, *auto-da-fé*. The sound patterns
conveyed significant unconscious content that fed the growth of
my unknown thought, which was made possible at once by my
patient's dream-text and departure from it. This is an effect of
what Lacan termed *lalangue*, a primitive and affective maternal

language which is largely unconscious (Lacan 1972–73, p. 126*f*). 'Typically,' writes Bollas,

> signifiers refer to other signifiers, establishing, as Lacan shows, the voice of the subject who speaks through these linked sounds. If the analyst receives the potential meaning of a word that bears other signifiers and if she sounds those words *spontaneously*, then the analyst's unconscious responds to the patient's unconscious in a dialogue of signifiers.
>
> (2009a, p. 50; emphasis in the original)

Psychoanalysts, Christopher Bollas reminds us, free associate. The Freudian *Einfall* specific to free association is not foreign to the analyst's inner experience. In fact, he argues that 'unconscious communication is enhanced if the analyst can disclose to the analysand mental contents of his own that are still unconscious, but seem of particular—and spontaneous—relevance to the reported mental contents of the analysand' (1992, p. 102). However, not all free associations are communicated because they do not seem to be 'related to the patient's material, to the transference, or to the emotional reality of the session' (1992, p. 113). The unknown thought possesses, in this case, an oneiric quality. Following Freud in 'The Unconscious' (1915b), Bollas thus suggests that 'the analyst free associates to his patient, drifting *away* through associative pathways of his own. . ., [which is] a kind of *countertransference dreaming'* (1995, p. 12; emphasis in the original).

How might I use these associations and fantasies in order to advance Marceline's treatment, to her self experience of analysis? Two operations were in order. I first had to understand that what was occurring between analysand and analyst was due to projective identification, by which the former places something dangerous or dreaded (or in some cases, something cherished) into the latter as a way of not only eliminating what is harmful or feared (or for safekeeping) but also object relating (Bollas 1987, p. 2 and 243). In Marceline's case, a mixed fear of abandonment by her boyfriend arousing hatred and desire for him was unbearable to her, and she made me feel this in my counter-transference. She was using me as a containing object for what was too painful but by which she could nevertheless regress. Her unconscious request was that I transform what was repressed into something that could become conscious. That, indeed, was why she had first come into analysis, even if at the time she was unaware of the true reasons for undertaking it. But there was another dimension of mental suffering that Marceline was presenting to me: her relationship to her distant mother and intrusive father, which preceded her love affair with her boyfriend and was its archaic paradigm, just as it was at this critical point in her psychoanalysis. She communicated this to me through the two means available to her at that moment, namely, dreaming and projective identification. Both combined elements of external and internal reality, the Covid-19 crisis and her relational crises past and present. In this regard, it seems likely that the temporary forcefulness of Marceline's dream and projective identification over me had something to do with the contagious potential of the virus; in other words, the patient's psyche was using both in tandem in order to infect the analyst with harmful particles (not unlike airborne droplets containing the virus) emanating from her unconscious mental life.

It was at this point that Marceline was communicating something important about her unthought known through her dream-text. The narrative was brief, and it seemed to evoke mainly manifest content related to Marceline's constraints due to the lockdown. This content was not to be ignored or diminished as it had to do with her present anguish. As to the curfew dream's latent content, it was not yet related by means of free association and interpretation to the unthought assumptions governing Marceline's early and later family environment, to her maternal and paternal orders. It was 'not yet mentally realised' but once it was, it would be possible to see that Marceline's dream was unconsciously figuring an ambivalent, and thus two-sided, deep-seated wish: on the one hand, she desired a man; on the other hand, she feared the harm a man could inflict, and so hated him. In her dream, the curfew was imposed from without, by the government. But her desire for a sexual relationship originated from within. The dream thus figured Marceline's reluctance to engage a man sexually, all the while wanting to do so regardless of whatever the government or any other external instance, parental, for instance, was imposing, which can be understood as a distortion of her own desire since the rationale for not undertaking a sexual relationship was attributed to an external instance. In other words, she was unconsciously telling me that it was she who was to blame for not being in a relationship, while she however placed the responsibility for her despair on another. The psychosexual politics expressed more or less manifestly through the dreamwork echoed Marceline's conflictual relationships with her parents whose beginnings could be traced to an unconsciously fantasised primal scene (Laplanche and Pontalis 1964/1985). This unconscious content needed to be communicated to her. Through our associative exchange, we came to understand that, for her, sex was a dirty (*sale*) virus, just as the politicians were bastards (*salauds*). She felt that in order to play it safe, she had to keep her distance from others, men in general. She seemed to repeat in her own way what her mother had done with regard to her family, husband and children alike. I suggested this to her in the third session when she again brought up her feelings about the politicians.

In the second session, however, something more of Marceline's libidinal crisis disclosed itself, once again in the transference catalysed by the move to prophylactic psychoanalysis. Her feelings of confusion about a sexual relationship with me, represented latently in the dream, were in accordance with her past relationships, notably the failed long-distance relationship, and they reflected this psychic history. It was further economically meaningful to observe how the drive was expressed in her transference now that the prophylactic analysis had begun: during the first session, she told me that she felt that talking on the telephone was disturbing because it reminded her of her earlier dissatisfactory relationship with her former boyfriend but also, implicitly, earlier on, those with her mother and father. This also explains why she was not opposed to the change in the setting when I first suggested it: she felt safer when far from me. This was interpreted in the third session, an interpretation that was first met defensively, by denial; but Marceline then admitted it might be true. I think that this shift had more to do with her greater capacity to think for herself, acquired in the course of her first two years of analysis, than with compliance to my interpretation. Be that as it may, interpretation of the transference not only exposed the pain of the earlier conflicts but brought them into relation with me. Unravelling the crisscrossing of her mental representations of elements external and internal to the analytic situation had the effect of diminishing her anxiety and further enabled her to see herself with greater clarity. Psychic genera had indeed been built up between us.

The viral Real had triggered the lifting of certain repressed material within Marceline's unconscious, to say nothing of mine. As we moved between object relations and subject relations, our respective and shared self experiences were undoubtedly affected by it. After this first week of working with Marceline prophylactically during which the transition from one setting to the other was occurring very quickly, it was clear that I needed to gather my thoughts together and reflect on how her unconscious conflict with her parents, her unthought known, emerged in the transference. As the experience of prophylactic analysis was as new to her as it was to me (although I did not tell her this), it needed to be worked through as much in the analytic situation as in my self-analysis, outside the liminal space. My clinical discussion is an attempt to account for how it unfolded.

4. 'Tuning in' in Viral Times

As this chapter concludes, I would like to sketch out some tentative thoughts on how the setting evolved in function of the viral Real. I was practicing prophylactic psychoanalysis and as such Marceline's analysis, for the time being, at least, no longer made use of the analytic mainstays, the couch and armchair, even if I sought to maintain the frequency of the sessions. What, then, was I to make of this variation of the setting? As I reflected on the modifications, I began to think about Bollas's remarks on the receptive unconscious as related to Freud's telephone metaphor, to how, that is, Freud compared psychoanalytic listening to the telephone receiver (Freud 1912c, p. 115–116). Freud, quoted by Bollas, writes that the analyst 'must turn his own unconscious like a receptive organ towards the transmitting unconscious of the patient. He must *adjust himself* to the transmitting microphone' (2007, p. 28, emphasis added; see also 1992, p. 95). Freud's choice of words—*zuwenden* ('to turn to') and *einstellen* ('to adjust,' 'to modulate' or 'to tune in') (Freud 1912b, p. 381)—makes clear the need for the analyst's listening—or unconscious perceptions—to be attuned to the patient's receptive unconscious emissions, even as it hovers or drifts across them. Need I understand this metaphor not only in relation to the receptive unconscious but also the dynamic unconscious? Need I further be restricted to taking the telephone receiver metaphor *literally*, that is, as merely metaphor? Or could there lie, behind the manifest metaphorical content, something latent, having an inner meaning? In thinking along these lines, I might come to an understanding that Marceline's prophylactic psychoanalysis was not an abandonment of the former setting but its temporary adaptation in order to try and satisfy the exigencies of a challenge raised by the new social and biological environment; in other words, it represented not so much a rupture with previous practice as its continuity. If the Freudian pair had been uncannily 'dislodged' from the conventional setting by the viral Real, it all the while remained in the psychoanalytic 'house' (Freud 1919).

Prophylactic psychoanalysis is a kind of provisional remote analysis that makes use of transmissive objects outside the conventional setting, while aiming specifically at impeding the virus's biological potential to spread. The question of the libidinal body within the liminal space of the psychic realm—perhaps *the* fundamental question concerning any form of multi-site analysis—receives a reply when we consider if self experience, psychoanalytically conceived, has in fact taken place.

In Marceline's case, prophylactic psychoanalysis did not impede dreaming and projective identification from occurring within the transference and leading to regressive states: the dreaming self 'had been there before' but the tie to what had been experienced previously lent it a specific colouring. 'Gathered and processed by the dream space and dream events, I live in a place where I seem to have been held before: inside the magical and erotic embrace of a forming intelligence that bears me' (Bollas 1992, p. 14). In particular, Bollas adds, the self's relation to the maternal is re-experienced. 'To be in a dream is thus a continuous reminiscence of being inside the maternal world when one was partly a receptive figure within a comprehending environment' (1992, p. 14). The dream involves a specific form of regression, topographical regression. 'In this respect the dream seems to be a structural memory of the infant's unconscious, an object relation of person inside the other's unconscious processing, revived in the continuous representation of the infantile moment every night' (1992, p. 14). The analysand's self, in short, continues to be experienced in specifically analytic terms.

The analyst's self experience likewise remained analytic. In the course of my self-analysis, I returned to my associations on the unconscious creativity of Marceline's curfew dream and how it aroused in me the *auto-da-fé* and burning of heretics. This was an expression of the moralistic urgings of my analytic superego faced with a possible betrayal of Freudian metapsychology and technique that I wished to respect. My dilemma, I told myself, was in a sense identical to Amelia's with regard to bowing. Prophylactic analysis was not only a necessary adjustment in the viral context but also permissible as a technique since it presented good-enough conditions to keep the analytic work alive. This required a de-idealisation of the classical setting. Freud, in fact, in using the telephone metaphor emphasises the need for the analyst to overcome his or her resistances in order to tune into how the patient's unconscious transmits (Freud 1912c, p. 116). It is further consistent with Winnicott's position regarding the facilitating environment, in which the analyst seeks to provide '*a live adaptation to the infant's needs*' (Winnicott 1960, p. 54; emphasis in the original).

In short, Marceline's prophylactic psychoanalysis would continue as long as required, until such a day when the 'brown fog of a winter dawn' clears from the sky; when my patient and I would—though of course it remained to be seen—return—as if any return to a departure point were possible—to the former, ordinary setting.

Chapter 6

Psychic Transformations

Air Hunger

Arthur C. Hurwitz, in memoriam

1. A Bicycle Ride

It is early April 2020. Several times a week now, since the French government put its lockdown measures into place and I no longer take the métro in order to minimise physical contact with others, I ride my bicycle to the hospital I work in. The journey lasts no more than about 20 minutes. It first takes me from the Avenue d'Italie to the Place d'Italie and down along the Boulevard de l'Hôpital, where I pass beside the Pitié-Salpêtrière Hospital on the way to the Austerlitz train station, across the Austerlitz bridge to the Right Bank and up along the Quai de la Rapée where I make a turn onto the Saint Martin Canal (where it joins the Seine), then up to the Place de la Bastille, beside the opera house, and finally from there a short way on the rue de Charenton to the 15–20 National Ophthalmology Hospital. There is little traffic, and so less pollution; only the occasional nearly empty city bus or automobile, delivery vehicle and motorcycle, along with cyclists like me.

Down I glide, then peddle onwards. Down to the river—called by the Romans—Sequana, which over the vast swaths of geological time has eroded a depression into the limestone, known as Lutetian after the Roman name of the city, forming several *buttes* on either side which Auden might have described, in 'In Praise of Limestone,' as 'From weathered outcrop/ To hill-top temple' (Auden 1948, p. 540). Down I go from the southern edge of the city, and then slightly upwards towards the Bastille.

DOI: 10.4324/9781003010999-7

The places and toponyms are of more recent origin: among them, the Pitié-Salpêtrière, founded in the second half of the seventeenth century by Louis XIV and where Freud as a visiting student observed Charcot's patients presenting hysteria; the Austerlitz train station and bridge which recall Napoléon's victory over the Russian and Austrian armies in December 1805; and the modern opera house designed by Carlos Ott and inaugurated by President François Mitterrand in 1989. Today's 15–20 Hospital, whose departments specialise in a range of common and rare ophthalmological illnesses and disorders, was built in the 1970s but its history goes far back: it was founded in the thirteenth century by Louis IX as a hospice for the blind among the Parisian poor as well soldiers returning from the conquest of Jerusalem with battle wounds to the eyes. How did it get its odd-sounding numerical name? The royal statutes made provisions for a population of 300, and 15×20 equals 300.

I spend mornings seeing the regularly hospitalised patients but also the Covid-19 patients we've taken on to relieve neighbouring hospitals of the torrent. The 15–20 does not have an intensive care unit (ICU). When the epidemic struck, however, it was decided that the hospital would open a sector to receive post-ICU patients requiring further care—mostly in the form of non-invasive oxygen therapy following acute dyspnea, hypoxia and pneumonia; physical therapy; and diet monitoring—before returning home. These patients no longer present life-threatening conditions. Some have a spouse in intensive care elsewhere or who is recently deceased due to the virus. They speak to me in these terse terms, only just on the verge of grieving: 'I learned that my wife was dying in the hospital when the ambulance picked me up and I was gasping for breath.' Another patient I see repeatedly for only brief interviews—all he can bear for the time being—had a tooth removed in order to facilitate intubation. When he awoke from the medically induced coma, he noticed it was missing. This of course occurred in another hospital. At this point, he only speaks about how much he's vexed because this particular tooth was used to anchor his denture. He cannot express any affect and appears indifferent to the month he was unconscious while on a ventilator. I observe him looking down at the floor and moving his hands around himself as if he were searching for the lost object (see also Bollas 2000, p. 117–126). It is a matter of a repetition compulsion in the face of unspoken traumatic experience—that of losing his breath and fearing it could not be found again; that of dying—which cannot yet be recalled and worked through. In short, I see these patients in order to try and help them elaborate something of their experiences, if they so wish, if they're ready (Jaron 2021).

The hospital room may be likened to what T.S. Eliot called a 'still point of the turning world' around which, were it not, there would be no 'dance' (Eliot 1936, p. 181). It is at this 'still point of the turning world' that patients speak, if they are able, of the terror of loss and death anxiety: loss of mothers and fathers, siblings and friends; the fear of dying and near brushes with death. Of what Bion calls nameless dread but also 'the will to live,' in reference to the model of an 'emotional situation in which the infant feels fear that it is dying,' that is, while at the mother's breast splitting off and projecting envy and hate, before reintrojecting a more 'tolerable' and 'growth-stimulating' element (Bion 1962a, p. 362*f*).

The hospital room, or rather what a psychoanalyst might do in it, comes to resemble this 'still point.' This makes sense to me because I do not think that what Eliot was thinking of is uniquely physical but also mental. As such, I contend that the analyst's mind, while in a state of negative capability or evenly hovering attentiveness, for example, likewise resembles the 'still point.' It is a kind of drawing inwards; not distancing oneself but opening up a psychic space which may receive or contain what is emitted, whether conscious or unconscious, from the patient's psyche. This is what makes it possible for me to continue to think and work as a psychoanalyst in a hospital setting.

The trip back to my office for my afternoon and evening sessions—all, now, conducted over the telephone or via a video platform—provides me with an additional view. Returning back onto the Austerlitz bridge, now heading south, offers a perspective of two landmarks: beyond the iron fence and gates enclosing the Jardin des Plantes, laid out in the first quarter of the seven-teenth century for the crown and where medicinal plants were (and are still) cultivated, I see off in the distance the great façade—constructed of limestone, in fact—of the Gallery of Evolution of the Museum of Natural History, founded just after the Revolution, but also, along the main path, the many flowering trees. Among them is a low-lying, sprawling Japanese cherry tree known as Kanzan. I've heard it said that if you visit Kanzan in early spring, while it's in full bloom for less than two weeks, it will bring you good luck for the coming year. (Some say, for three years.) From afar, beyond the closed gates of the garden—it's off-limits due to the epidemic—I picture the thousands of ephemeral, tightly packed, light-pink flowers, at once delicate and mighty, and I think to myself, with regret but also hope projected into the future: 'Not this year, perhaps the next.'

From the Jardin des Plantes, I slowly peddle back up the Boule-vard de l'Hôpital, stopping once at a traffic light to catch my breath and conscious of the effort I have to make before reaching the top of the hill at the Place d'Italie. My mind considers the relationship between the natural world studied in the garden and the Covid-19 virus that has shaken the world's population, sowing uncertainty, fear and death across it. Winded as I am, though, I'm also forced to ask if I myself have been infected or rather if it's merely a case of post-winter flaccidity.

Christopher Bollas recalls Gaston Bachelard's topoanalysis and Guy Debord's psycho-geography (1998, p. 54 and 77)—Debord in particular speaks of a *dérive* or 'drifting' through an urban landscape—to account for the subjective appropriating of external spaces and the objects that fill them. It is a matter of not only space but also time. In the course of my short bicycle ride, I pass through a jumble of geological, natural, political and cul-tural history stretching across at least 250 million years ago up through the present. The past suffuses the present and as such the narrative is only linear in a manifest way. In fact, it's less a nar-rative than an oneiric production, similar to what Bollas terms a *dream-text* described as a 'primordial fiction' (1987, p. 68). In a psychoanalysis, the analysand 'lingers with the dream-text, borrowing its form, and talking without knowing much of what this means' (Bollas 2002, p. 44). I am not indifferent to this history; in some ways, gradually over time, I have made it my own. I *linger* with it, and so its outward linearity of the history breaks apart as my unconscious mentation articulates it (Bollas 2007, p. 62). Somewhere in the mental background to my bicycles ride is set my unthought known, an infinite quantity of unconscious assumptions which I have not yet brought into my conscience but which formed during my infancy and the early years of my childhood. The objects I encounter along the journey have less objective meaning to me, even if their external reality may be defined, than that deep subjectivity through which my own idiom and character are expressed. These objects possess a 'processional potential' each of which awakens in me 'a different form of subjective transformation' (Bollas 1992, p. 5) due to their integrity and distinctiveness. They are fundamentally part of my self experience cast adrift.

While lingering, or drifting, something 'primordial' awakens in my conscious mind as I cross the Austerlitz bridge travelling from the southern half of the city northwards to the hospital. In the interstitial space connecting the Left Bank to the Right Bank, the spring sun is relatively low and the air is cool in the morning (it is early in the season) and it sets itself upon me from the right side, warming me a little for a precious few seconds, as it rises in the east. I then look to the left and see Notre Dame Cathedral, also largely built of limestone, still bearing the traces of flame from the fire that ravaged it from within a year earlier. A mechanical crane towers over it, tall and thin, like the great bird from which it takes its name, with its long neck stretched out and its eyes gazing downwards into a pond. As my own gaze is captured by this unprobable scene and my thoughts are overtaken by it—Lautréamont's 'chance juxtaposition of a sewing machine and an umbrella on a dissecting table' crosses my mind (Lautréamont 1869, p. 322), as does Bachelard's *Psychoanalysis of Fire* (1949)—am I unconsciously thinking of the Covid-19 patients, also ravaged by fire from within, surrounded by mechanical apparatuses keeping them alive?

As I look out towards the left, I see myself riding my bicycle, not as in a mirror but my outline on the asphalt, object casting shadow. There arises in my consciousness the image of a painting, Francis Bacon's 1966 portrait of George Dyer riding a bicycle, its front wheel fractured into perhaps three and Dyer's darkened profile figured within, which is part of a deformed face viewed frontally. It's been suggested that the deformed face within the silhouette is Bacon himself (Harrison 2016, vol. 3, p. 824), in which case that the 'Portrait of George Dyer' is at once a portrait of Dyer and a self-portrait; or, more precisely, a depiction of how Bacon perceives Dyer imagining his lover, the painting's painter.

I've made this trip now many times and, as I think about it, I've come to understand that the intersecting of historical moments as I move along the trajectory resemble, in their own way, what's depicted in the Dyer portrait. There is kinesis, or rather its illusion (the front wheel is an oval); and a shadowed profile turned inwards containing the deformed features of a head whose gaze is directed outwards. It's impossible to know which gaze—the inward or the outward—to privilege. The continuous shifting of perspectives occurs simultaneously, as if time stood outside time, a timelessness of unconscious processes Freud writes of in *The Interpretation of Dreams*: 'it is a prominent feature of unconscious processes that they are indestructible. In the unconscious nothing can be brought to an end, nothing is past or forgotten' (Freud 1900, p. 577). And further, in the chapters on metapsychology: 'The processes of the system *Ucs* are timeless; i.e., they are not ordered temporally, are not altered by the passage of time; they have no reference to time at all. Reference to time is bound up . . . with the work of the system *Cs*' (Freud 1915b, p. 187). Within the unconscious, Freud reflected as the Great War raged, there could be no representation of one's own death (Freud 1915c, p. 296). And yet. . .

Within the liminal space of the Austerlitz bridge connecting the Left Bank to the Right Bank, I'm at once outside time and within it. I'm aware that I'm at a 'still point' and my reverie—this free-floating, awakened intrapsychic mentation—is but a way of coping with the clinical work I try to maintain in a time of upheaval. This psychic work is eminently therapeutic, and it's something indispensable that I take into my clinical practice.

2. Pierre-Maxime

Psychoanalysis is a motor for affecting what Christopher Bollas has termed *psychic transformations*, which can occur in even a very brief encounter, as in a hospital room. In this setting, the patient, left to linger around his or her free associations, is as subject to transformations of the psyche in relation to the analyst as transformational object as any other in the ordinary consulting room. Bollas states that the 'infinite combination of growing thought is . . . Freud's core theory of the unconscious and clearly a model of mental development' (2007, p. 17). In this particular case, a shared sense of illusion, such as that described by Winnicott (Winnicott 1971, p. 11), shifts between playing and reality; it contains, in various degrees, elements of both. And this operation occurs very quickly, almost instantaneously as it is established between patient and analyst.

It is the third week of April and Kanzan has not had any admirers this year other than the gardeners. Its annual bloom, the cyclical transience, has run its course, the tiny, explosive (to the eyes) pink flowers having fallen silently to the ground around a week earlier.

Pierre-Maxime has been in our Covid-19 unit for two days. He had received an endotracheal intubation and was on ventilation while in a medically induced coma for three weeks followed by one week out of the coma in a nearby hospital. He is now undergoing oxygen therapy and seeing the physical therapist and nutritionist daily. I should add that Pierre-Maxime's hospitalisation in our post-intensive-care unit occurs while the number of sick appears to be reaching its peak. During the morning staff meeting, in which the self within the working of the *group mind* is sensed to its fullest (2013a, p. 97), information from the night shift team is relayed, the patients' physical and moral progress is discussed, and admissions and discharges are noted. An ultrasound carried out by the cardiologist or a visit by the social worker might be scheduled. For each, the necessary dose of litres of oxygen per minute and at what percentage is calculated. I imagine that this is something like the feeding of an infant. Indeed, in the best of cases, a patient will be *sevré*, 'weaned,' from oxygen therapy. We gather at a table for a cup of coffee, masks lowered and dangling from an ear or around the neck, the requisite distance between each of us respected. While I'm humbled by my colleagues' ethical sensibility and courage translated seemingly without thinking into both simple and complicated acts of care, I'm also conscious of their vulnerability. I ask how everyone is doing. There are polite smiles. No one dares to go into the details but once home in the evening I am certain that some will break down while on their couches. The exchange continues. The attending physician asks me to see a particular patient, a man in his late 20s, because he wishes to talk about what has happened to him. My colleague adds perspicaciously, a month after we'd opened this unit, that she's observing a change in how the patients in general are doing mentally: 'We're now seeing patients who have been in intensive care for four or five weeks. They know that their cases are serious.'

I leave the staff room, walk down the hall and enter Pierre-Maxime's room, introducing myself. He says that he's happy to see me. As he speaks, he's making a clumsy, half-hearted attempt at buttoning his gown from behind his neck but is having trouble (or wishes to appear so, I say to myself) and asks if I might help him. The request is awkward but since he's partially naked and I'm in full protective clothing, I go over to him and button the button. Perhaps this is his way of asking if he can trust me while in the depths of his vulnerability, if he can feel relaxed in my presence (Winnicott 1971, p. 55). From the start he's trying to seduce.

'I've just come out of the shower. It's the first one I've taken by myself since I fell ill.' He's visibly satisfied with himself, even if he hasn't washed his hair because his arms are too weak to lift them above his head. And then: 'I'd like to tell you about where I'm from.' The statement intrigues me, as it demonstrates a certain reflective detachment, all the while showing a satisfactory narcissistic interest in himself. It also seems to be a bit of theatre while still grounded in reality. Most importantly, a request to be listened to has been made. I ask myself if the apparent levity of the buttoning episode, behind the wish to seduce, might not mask something more serious. What lies behind the request?

I go and sit down in an armchair and say, mirroring him: 'Tell me about where you're from.' Pierre-Maxime smiles, ready, it seems, to play because he senses that I too am ready to join in the game. If I reply in a way that confirms his wish to play, this is a response that is perhaps not entirely unconscious on my part; rather as one goes to the waiting room to take a child into the office, the potential for play is always present. Yet the attending physician's remarks remain in my thoughts. They remind me that playing can figure something sinister behind which lies, for instance, primitive anxiety. The patient appears stable but perhaps he fears breaking down. If the initial transferential dynamic is in fact eroticised, then to Eros is fused a measure of Thanatos.

From the chair beside the bed, I look at Pierre-Maxime lying back, his hands clasping each other and set upon his stomach. His skin appears dry and pale, and his eyes are slightly sunken. He tells me, while he's beginning to feel a little better physically despite the muscle atrophy, that he'd like to talk. He was in touch with his family and friends as well as many colleagues in the engineering firm where he works. Everyone he knows had been concerned about his health. There is, however, something that he characterises as 'delirious' and that he can't quite get past. I ask him to tell me about it. The period in question was the transitional week or so when he'd come out of the coma and progressively regained full consciousness. He has no recollection of being in the coma and only little of what happened just before he was put into it. 'I couldn't breathe, I was sure that I was going to lose consciousness.' And then nothing, he'd 'slid over the edge.' He adds that his family had written him a letter, which they asked the medical personnel to read at his bedside. He's not quite sure what the letter contained but thinks that it was a list of everyone's name in his family, telling him that they were all present for him. I wonder why he had not yet read this letter. Had the staff neglected to give it to him before he left the hospital? I keep this question to myself.

A first association then comes to my mind: the violinist Paul Robertson's remarkable recounting of lying in a coma for many weeks after suffering a ruptured aorta, during which he occasionally experienced 'visions' characterised as 'horrific,' 'plainly psychotic,' or 'exquisitely beautiful' (Robertson 2016, p. 7). Were Pierre-Maxime's visions similar? I turn back to listening.

He has only a vague notion of the short time before he was extubated and brought out of the coma. He feels that he heard his father's voice, though he did not understand what he was saying. Then he was no longer in the coma. His head was heavy and he felt as if it were filled with fog; he was not sure of where he was. He could not move his arms or legs. Eating and drinking were out of the question as he could not swallow and feared choking on food and liquids. He was greatly helped by the nurses and orderlies for all his needs. As he lay in bed, he continued to hear his father's voice, which became clearer to him. It was a hypnopompic production which he tried to make sense of. The father came from another country, he says. I ask to him elaborate. 'It's strange,' he thinks, adding that he had come out of the coma only a few days before his father's birthday. His father was then dead for some years but he could hear his voice. He repeats that this is 'delirium,' all the while convinced of its veracity: it was not as if he had imagined it; it was the voice itself. Perhaps it represented a kind of birth, he thinks. He believes that life and death, or becoming born and dying, are conjoined. What was he telling him? Pierre-Maxime explains that his father had a reputation in the family for his knowledge of the folk traditions of his homeland. His father told a story about a simple water carrier who falls in love with a married noblewoman, and she with him, and then sang a song about a baby, one of the king's sons, admired by all. I look at him calmly, and he returns my gaze. I see him thinking.

I'm struck by how he's relating to me. His free, associative way of speaking to a complete stranger intrigues me and I tell him so. He explains that he had been in psychoanalysis before while doing his engineering degree. The experience had been beneficial: it enabled him to complete his studies and find a job, and he accepted having a woman in his life. He tells me that he feels my presence like that of his analyst. The transferential motion is palpable. His receptivity to play even as I walked into his room then makes sense to me. His unthought known might be sensed in this playful scene, though I do not know yet its basic terms. My countertransferential unknown thought, however, receives it as our respective unconsciouses communicate with each other.

Many individuals in his entourage had been deeply worried about his health. The firm's director had informed him that once he could check his e-mail account again, he was going to be inundated with messages of concern from colleagues throughout the world. I ask him how he feels about this. His gaze changes as he looks at me straight in the eye. He's silent. He can't find the words to describe his feelings. I ask him if he's troubled by all this concern. He's still silent. I wait for a moment and then offer an interpretation of his silence in which I affirm his initial utterance. 'You've come from afar, like your father. You didn't know if you were going to make it. You've pulled through.'

His eyes become wet. Seeing him cry and taking in the measure of his depleted physical while talking about his colleagues, I see in my mind freed prisoners having returned from the Nazi camps. They are gathered at the Hôtel Lutetia along the boulevard Raspail following the liberation of Paris. Around them are family members seeking news about the deported. I do not communicate this association to him—at bottom, it is irrelevant to him—but rather develop an interpretation that arises out of the associative matrix: 'You see yourself as a survivor.'

He takes a deep breath.

PATIENT: Yes I do. I might have gone. It's strange but just before all this happened, my wife and I had spoken about having a child. It seemed like the right time for both of us. Now we'll carry on from where we left off.

ANALYST: 'But you've been changed by this experience.'

PATIENT: 'Yes I have.' He pauses. 'I think I understand now what is bothering me so much. I'm not sure if the others, despite all their concern, can ever understand what I've gone through.'

Again he's silent. He then says that calling him a survivor is quite apposite, and in an uncanny way.

ANALYST: 'How so?'

I look at him, my gaze prompting him to continue. He stares right back at me while telling me that a generation earlier a large part of his wife's family had been caught up in a genocide. Many had been murdered, a few had survived. His wife had always been struck by how little they had said about their experiences. He is perfectly aware of the reticence of many survivors to talk about what they'd been through, either for lack of understanding it themselves or out of fear of being misunderstood by others. The reticence might last decades; the silence, a lifetime. And so while he's sceptical as to whether his family and colleagues could ever understand him, he's nevertheless certain that his consciousness had altered indelibly.

Pierre-Maxime's father comes back to mind.

ANALYST: 'Your father was speaking to you. Speaking about himself to you.' He agrees.

PATIENT: 'My father gave me my voice.'

Perhaps, at some point, he'll find the courage to talk to others. He'd wished to speak to me. But at present, he's unsure how he'd tell them just what he feels about surviving his illness. It's simply too soon to do so.

This initial meeting has come to an end and I ask him if he'd like me to visit him again. He'd like that very much. I rise and leave the room.

I see him two days later. His muscles still feel 'mushy,' and his head is not yet 'right.' In the *après-coup* of our initial encounter, two images have come to mind. He's unsure when the first one occurred to him, if it was as his respiratory system was decompensating before being hospitalised or perhaps even during the coma. He imagined four washcloths hanging from a garland. The washcloths shimmer with many colours. I ask him what the image makes him think of.

PATIENT: 'It's as if the four washcloths represented my lungs, the four lobes of my lungs. And the sparkling colours were all germs.'

I think to myself, 'There are five lobes: the anatomy of the right lung consists of three.' It goes without saying that I'm not out to correct him; rather, I sense that the error might be meaningful, as such distortions sometimes are, and that it's better to wait and see if other associations are made. Further, he doesn't associate on the garland.

While these thoughts are moving through my mind, Pierre-Maxime tells me about the second image that had occurred to him.

The note that my family sent to read: again, I'm not sure if this idea came to me during the coma or just afterwards but I think it was an ex-voto, the kind you see in churches. The note was taped onto the wall of my room.

I ask him if he can say something more.

My wife and I travel when we can, and we often visit churches. We're not religious but they're beautiful. Part of their beauty comes from the ex-votos. People put them there as signs of recognition that something terrible had happened but that they'd made it through.

I suggest to him that he doesn't feel that what had happened to him was a matter of a visit to a beautiful church. Somewhere inside he

felt deeply frightened and, at present, perhaps relieved. He thinks
so, too. I ask him why he didn't take the letter with him when he
was discharged. 'You don't remove an ex-voto from a church.'
After admitting that it is somewhat out of his character to express
thanks, he adds that he was indeed deeply grateful to the others
who had helped him. The healthcare institution (the mother) had
not failed him (the infant) in his distress (with regard to feeding)
(see Bion 1962a, p. 299f). Nor is his analyst, he feels at present.

I end the session there and tell him I'll come by at the beginning
of the following week.

A final exchange occurs. Pierre-Maxime has recovered enough
to justify leaving the hospital and will be going home that very
day. Another blank troubles him, the period between returning
from a hiking trip when he was feverish and experiencing acute
respiratory distress leading up to hospitalisation in the ICU. He
recounts: 'There's no trace of this time, either in my mind or my
body.' He found some messages exchanged during this period on
his telephone but can recall nothing about them. He thinks that the
amnesia was induced by encephalitic fever or, possibly, traumatic
shock. Once he is back home, talking to his wife and sleeping in
his bed again after five weeks, he might recall something of the
time. His only certainty is that he feared dying. He then remem-
bers something: 'I saw myself as a drone hovering over a scene,
my family below. I was observing how they were reacting to my
departure.' I ask him how they feel. 'They're filled with sadness.
Their love is very great.' He explains that well before contracting the virus, he had already imagined such a scene. This time,
however, 'It was real' and, he thinks, crying, perhaps he had in
fact died. Now, he feels, 'It's like a renaissance.' He's restored to
life, breathing.

He returns to the wish to have children but speaks about his
mother who, he had learned, had closely followed all the reports
concerning his status while in the ICU. His wife told him that
'she was very rational about the whole thing,' with one excep-
tion: 'She'd prayed, in her own way (not being religious), to my
father to do anything possible to see me through the ordeal.' For

his mother, 'It was out of the question that her child might die before she did.' I ask him why he associated having children and his mother. He turns inwards, then outwards: 'It's her birthday in two days.' Transgenerational maternal and paternal orders dialogue effortlessly while expressing desire.

I ask about the children. I'm surprised to hear that he and his wife would like to have four, 'either naturally or through adoption'; surprised, because that is the number of 'lobes' he had imagined. He doesn't evoke this image. Perhaps he finds it too disturbing, as the lungs, even if they were hanging from a garland, were filled with germs. I sense a nascent conflict concerning the wish to have children. He's on the point of leaving the hospital, and it won't be possible to explore this question. I tell him that he can come to see me once the hospital is scheduling regular outpatient consultations once more, or that he may phone me later on if he wishes to. I then leave his room a final time.

Pierre-Maxime and I have only started to produce the psychic fibre that can be woven into a meaningful, though doubtless still incomplete representation of what had occurred to him. The work is unfinished but now he's returning home. It's an established fact that a psychoanalysis may be interrupted at any moment, that contingencies are always present. He will, however, surely continue his psychic work on his own. Perhaps he'll view these last weeks as a dream, and in particular the three weeks of coma: while, as Damasio says, being in a coma is not, neurologically, the equivalent to sleeping (Damasio 2000, p. 236–237), the days before the crisis led to the hospitalisation could then be thought of as the moment parents insist, against the child's will, on putting out the lights at bedtime, with all the anxiety this arouses; and the days afterwards as a period of awakening bearing the traces of sleep when dream images are sometimes produced. I do not know. Perhaps he'll wish to forget them entirely. Or, on the contrary, perhaps he'll be unable to. And, further, to what extent had he consciously experienced the coma? There was no recollection of it, save, he thought, something hardly represented which occurred just before he regained consciousness. Mind had effectively left body, and the psychosomatic unity had been artificially defused leading to a momentary absence of representation and affect. To this was added nameless dread: the fear of dying and not being understood afterwards. Concerning the former, Pierre-Maxime was in the process of working through it, even if significant traces remained; as to the latter, at the time of the sessions, he seems to have resigned himself to this fate. Perhaps this position would evolve later in time. I recall Winnicott's summary of fear of breakdown in this regard:

> I have attempted to show that fear of breakdown can be a fear of a past event that has not yet been experienced. The need to experience it is equivalent to a need to remember in terms of the analysis of psycho-neurotics.
>
> This idea can be applied to other allied fears, and I have mentioned the fear of death and the search for emptiness.
>
> (Winnicott 1963, p. 95)

I further weigh what Bollas says with regard to the writings of the historian but likewise the reconstructions of the psychoanalyst:

> Reviewing the past, retrieving finite details from it and giving them new, indeed, contemporary meanings, detraumatises the subject who suffers from the ailments of many a thing done. By making past events meaningful, the historian exercises an important psychic capacity, that of reflection: this does not confer retrospective truth on the past—indeed, almost the contrary—but creates a new meaning that did not exist before, or that could not exist were it not based on past events and did it not transform them into a tapestry holding them in a new place ....
>
> (1995, p. 143)

As I'm going over these sessions while writing out some notes, and as I reread Winnicott on breakdown and Bollas on the psychically transformative power of reflection, I tell myself that working with Pierre-Maxime could be thought of as the microcosm of a greater psychoanalysis. I hear Blake: 'To see a World in a Grain of Sand' (Blake 1803, p. 295). A psychoanalysis in miniature, then, which convened a Freudian pair, Pierre-Maxime and me. An unusually brief psychoanalysis, lasting only three sessions spread out over a week or so during which a request had been made, a transferential–countertransferential dynamic established, and unconscious fear and desire explored and partially worked through against the backdrop of a traumatic experience arousing primitive anxiety and with the support of the analyst's interpretations—albeit in an unconventional setting adapted to the patient's needs. Is there any psychoanalysis that is not unalloyed in some way? Most importantly, breakdown may have loomed but it had been averted, at least temporarily. I laugh under my breath when I consider that this analytic cure surely has the distinction of being the shortest in the history of French psychoanalysis.

The interpretation I gave in which I called Pierre-Maxime a survivor—an interpretation that Bollas would designate as a known thought—was made possible for at least two reasons: first, because he implicitly presented his father as such and narcissistically associated himself with him; and second, because out of my countertransferential unknown thought I had related the image of returned prisoners at the Hôtel Lutetia to the limestone called Lutetian by the Romans, and further to the poem by Auden in which that particular stone is praised. These two factors coalesced in my mind and gave rise to the interpretation, which seemingly had a therapeutic effect of producing psychic genera. Pierre-Maxime reflected on the interpretation, and he associated it with the fortunes of a part of his wife's family who'd also survived. His identification with them enabled him to clarify something that, till then, had troubled him; namely, how he felt about making it through and how his entourage would subsequently view him. He anticipated, despite their goodwill, that they would not be able to understand and that the Covid-19 experience, that is, what was specific to his self experience while ill and recovering, would henceforth set him apart.

While I'm setting out these thoughts, my bicycle rides to and from the hospital come to mind. I tell myself that the psychic work in the *après-coup* that Pierre-Maxime will carry out in his own way bears a certain resemblance to the free associating my mind is engaged in when I'm out riding. Both are salutary, a breath of fresh air and a means to psychic growth, whether confronting oneself with what is most difficult or not. When the unconscious makes connections, it creates: it carries out a work of binding and reworks a traumatic past into something new, something relatively free of painful charges of affect. Words may then replace acts.

Here, I must explain briefly why I've chosen to call my patient 'Pierre-Maxime.' Attributing a pseudonym to a patient discussed with others either orally or in print is but one necessary alternation—Bion would speak in terms of 'distortion' (Bion 1967, p. 162*f*), or a movement from 'so-called clinical reports' to 'verbal transformations of sensory impressions' (Bion 1967, p. 200)—of the factual and emotional elements comprising the analytic environment indispensable to respecting individual privacy (Bollas and Sundelson 1995, p. 186*f*). One might add that there are times when the link between the fictitious name and the patient is quite conscious in the analyst's mind. In the previous chapters, the violinist Amelia is a disciple (in French, *émule*); the French pronunciation of the letter 'h' in the name of Mme H approximates that of the English word, 'ash' (an echo of her mother's ashes in the urn) and 'ash' is further a homophone of the French for 'axe' (*hache*), which recalls how her ponytail had been cut off as a young girl; naming the blind schizophrenic Lucien evokes the Latin for 'light' (*lux*); and Marceline is an allusion to the poet, Marceline Desbordes-Valmore. By means of such transformations, the patient's identity is veiled while elements of the analyst's unknown thought are disclosed.

As to Pierre-Maxime, I might have called him Arthur, Rimbaud's first name. Like Rimbaud, Pierre-Maxime went through his season in hell after he'd 'swallowed a mouthful of poison' and felt his 'guts burn' (Rimbaud 1873, p. 99–100) during which, like the poet, he experienced 'delirium,' first recounting that of one of his 'companions of hell' (Verlaine, possibly) and then a series of his own (Rimbaud 1873, p. 102–112). Arthur, however, is the given name of my friend to whom these thoughts are dedicated and I feel it inappropriate to assimilate him to Rimbaud. (He, however, might very well have given his approval. This I cannot know.) What's more important to me, I suppose, is how I associate 'Pierre' with limestone (in French, *calcaire*; but once again I am thinking across languages). That's evident enough. It then occurs to me that limestone is no longer quarried in Paris but extracted from the area around Saint-Maximin, a town north of Paris in the Oise. When I query myself—and querying is a form of quarrying—I cannot say how I know this nor why I made the connection between 'Maxime' and the name of the area where limestone has been quarried since the nineteenth century, when extraction was no longer possible in and around Paris as the city grew. Perhaps I learned this when, many years ago, I lived in the north of France and worked as an English teacher in a school. After all, the mind has an odd way of retaining and assembling bits and pieces of minute, seemingly insignificant local knowledge (Bion's K activity) that stay dormant for ages and then, as if they needed air to breathe and so quickly emerge from below to open space, suddenly awaken to consciousness.

The underlying intention of psychoanalytic treatment, we then find, is to uncover a particular form of knowledge, that is, how we live absorbed in 'nowness' while we are invariably bound to the underlying logic of the unthought known by the unconscious's tenacious embrace.

Bibliography

Auden, W.H. (1948). In Praise of Limestone. In *Collected Poems*. Edward Mendelson (editor). New York: Vintage, 1991, p. 540–542.

Bach, J.S. (1720). *Sonaten und Partiten für Violine allein*. Facsimile of the autograph manuscript. Günter Haußwald (afterword). Leipzig: Insel, 1958.

Bachelard, Gaston (1949). *La psychanalyse du feu*. Paris: Gallimard.

Balint, Michael (1932). Character Analysis and New Beginning. In *Primary Love and Psycho-Analytic Technique*. London: Hogarth and the Institute of Psycho-Analysis, 1952, p. 159–173.

Balint, Michael (1968). *The Basic Fault: Therapeutic Aspects of Regression*. London: Tavistock.

Bartók, Béla (1947). *Sonata for Solo Violin*. London: Boosey and Hawkes, 1994.

Bion, W.R. (1940). The 'War of Nerves': Civilian Reaction, Morale and Prophylaxis. In *The Complete Works of W.R. Bion*, volume 4. Chris Mawson (editor). London: Karnac, 2014, p. 5–21.

Bion, W.R. (1962a). *Learning from Experience*. In *The Complete Works of W.R. Bion*, volume 4. Chris Mawson (editor). London: Karnac, 2014, p. 259–365.

Bion, W.R. (1962b). A Theory of Thinking. In *Second Thoughts: Selected Papers on Psycho-Analysis* (1967). In *The Collected Works of W.R. Bion*, volume 6. Chris Mawson (editor). London: Karnac, 2014, p. 153–161.

Bion, W.R. (1967). *Second Thoughts: Selected Papers on Psychoanalysis*. In *The Complete Works of W.R. Bion*, volume 6. Chris Mawson (editor). London: Karnac, 2014, p. 53–202.

Bion, W.R. (1968–69). Further Cogitations. In *The Complete Works of W.R. Bion*, volume 15. Chris Mawson (editor). London: Karnac, 2014, p. 61–88.

Bion, W.R. (1970). *Attention and Interpretation: A Scientific Approach to Insight in Psycho-Analysis and Groups*. In *The Complete Works of W.R. Bion*, volume 6. Chris Mawson (editor). London: Karnac, 2014, p. 221–330.

Bion, W.R. (1977). *The Tavistock Seminars*. In *The Complete Works of W.R. Bion*, volume 9. Chris Mawson (editor). London: Karnac, 2014, p. 7–92.

Blake, William (1803). *Auguries of Innocence*. In *Selected Poems*. G.E. Bentley (editor). London: Penguin, 2005, p. 295–298.

Bollas, Christopher (1974). Character: The Language of Self. *International Journal of Psychoanalytic Psychotherapy* (number 3), p. 397–418.

Bollas, Christopher (1976). Le langage secret de la mère et de l'enfant. Claude Monod (translator). *Nouvelle Revue de Psychanalyse* (number 14), p. 241–246.

Bollas, Christopher (1978). The Aesthetic Moment and the Search for Transformation. *The Annual of Psychoanalysis* (number 6), p. 385–394.

Bollas, Christopher (1982). Review of André Green, *The Tragic Effect*. *International Journal of Psycho-Analysis* (volume 9), p. 109–111.

Bollas, Christopher (1987). *The Shadow of the Object: Psychoanalysis of the Unthought Known*. London: Free Association.

Bollas, Christopher (1989a). *Forces of Destiny: Psychoanalysis and Human Idiom* (2nd edition). London and New York: Routledge, 2019.

Bollas, Christopher (1989b). Portrait d'une personnalité psychanalytique peu ordinaire. Michel Gribinski (translator). *Nouvelle Revue de Psychanalyse* (number 40), p. 335–338.

Bollas, Christopher (1992). *Being a Character: Psychoanalysis and Self Experience*. Hove and New York: Routledge.

Bollas, Christopher (1995). *Cracking Up: The Work of Unconscious Experience*. New York: Farrar, Straus and Giroux.

Bollas, Christopher (1998). Architecture and the Unconscious. In *The Evocative Object World*. London and New York: Routledge, 2009, p. 47–77.

Bollas, Christopher (1999). *The Mystery of Things*. London and New York: Routledge.

Bollas, Christopher (2000). *Hysteria*. London and New York: Routledge.

Bollas, Christopher (2002). Free Association. In *The Evocative Object World*. London and New York: Routledge, 2009, p. 5–45.

Bollas, Christopher (2005). The Fourth Object and Beyond. In *The Evocative Object World*. London and New York: Routledge, 2009, p. 95-113.

Bollas, Christopher (2006a). *Mayhem*. London: Free Association.

Bollas, Christopher (2006b). *Theraplay and Other Plays*. London: Free Association.

Bollas, Christopher (2007). *The Freudian Moment*. London: Karnac.

Bollas, Christopher (2009a). *The Infinite Question*. London and New York: Routledge.

Bollas, Christopher (2009b). *The Evocative Object World*. London and New York: Routledge.

Bollas, Christopher (2011a). Character and Interformality. In *The Christopher Bollas Reader*. Arne Jemstedt (introduction) and Adam Phillips (foreword). London and New York: Routledge, p. 238–248.

Bollas, Christopher (2011b). The Wisdom of the Dream. In *The Christopher Bollas Reader*. Arne Jemstedt (introduction) and Adam Phillips (foreword). London and New York: Routledge, p. 249–258.

Bollas, Christopher (2011c). Introduction to Jonathan Sklar. In *Landscapes of the Dark: History, Trauma, Psychoanalysis*. London: Karnac, p. xv–xxiii.

Bollas, Christopher (2013a). *China on the Mind*. London and New York: Routledge.

Bollas, Christopher (2013b). *Catch Them before They Fall: The Psychoanalysis of Breakdown*. Followed by a conversation with Sacha Bollas. London and New York: Routledge.

Bollas Christopher (2015a). *When the Sun Bursts: The Enigma of Schizophrenia*. New Haven and London: Yale University Press.

Bollas, Christopher (2015b). André. *Revue française de psychanalyse* (volume 79, number 3), p. 836–839.

Bollas, Christopher (2018a). *Meaning and Melancholia: Life in the Age of Bewilderment*. London and New York: Routledge.

Bollas, Christopher (2018b). Materialising the Unthought Known: Reflections on the Work of Anish Kapoor. In *Anish Kapoor—Obras, pensamentos, experiências/Works, Thoughts, Experiments*. Porto: Museu de Arte Contemporânea de Serralves, p. 235–247.

Bollas, Christopher (2021a). Foreword to Nina Coltart. In *The Baby and the Bathwater*. Oxford: Phoenix, p. xiii–xviii.

Bollas, Christopher (2021b). Civilization and the Discontented. In *Psychoanalysis and Covidian Life: Common Distress, Individual*

Experience. Howard B. Levine and Ana de Staal (editors). Oxford: Phoenix, p. 3–21.

Bollas, Christopher (2021c). *Three Characters: Narcissist, Borderline, Manic Depressive*. Followed by a conversation with Sacha Bollas. Oxford: Phoenix.

Bollas, Christopher and David Sundelson (1995). *The New Informants: Betrayal of Confidentiality in Psychoanalysis and Psychotherapy*. London: Karnac.

Bowie, Malcolm (1991). *Lacan*. London: Fontana.

Chabert, Catherine (2003). *Féminin mélancolique*. Paris: Presses universitaires de France.

Coltart, Nina E.C. (1985). 'Slouching towards Bethlehem' . . . Thinking the Unthinkable in Psychoanalysis. In *The British School of Psychoanalysis: The Independent Tradition*. Gregorio Kohon (editor). London: Free Association, 1986, p. 185–199.

Damasio, Antonio (2000). *The Feeling of What Happens: Body, Emotion and the Making of Consciousness*. London: Vintage.

Demény, János (editor) (1971). *Béla Bartók: Letters*. London: Faber and Faber.

Dickinson, Emily (1863). *The Poems of Emily Dickinson* (Variorum edition). R.W. Franklin (editor). Cambridge, Massachusetts and London: The Belknap Press of Harvard University Press, 1998, p. 552–553.

Eliot, T.S. (1922). *The Waste Land. The Poems of T.S. Eliot: Collected and Uncollected Poems*, volume 1. Christopher Ricks and Jim McCue (editors). London: Faber and Faber, 2015, p. 53–77.

Eliot, T.S. (1936). *Burnt Norton. The Poems of T.S. Eliot: Collected and Uncollected Poems*, volume 1. Christopher Ricks and Jim McCue (editors). London: Faber and Faber, 2015, p. 179–184.

Eliot, T.S. (1940). *East Coker. The Poems of T.S. Eliot: Collected and Uncollected Poems*, volume 1. Christopher Ricks and Jim McCue (editors). London: Faber and Faber, 2015, p. 185–192.

Fabian, Dorottya (2015). *A Musicology of Performance: Theory and Method Based on Bach's Solos for Violin*. Cambridge: Open Book.

Fass, Egbert (1971). Ted Hughes and Crow. *London Magazine* (new series, volume 10, number 10), p. 5–20.

Ferenczi, Sándor (1928). The Elasticity of Psycho-Analytic Technique. In *Final Contributions to the Problems and Methods of Psycho-Analysis*. Michael Balint (editor). London: Hogarth and the Institute of Psycho-Analysis, p. 87–101.

Freud, Sigmund (1900). *The Interpretation of Dreams. SE* volumes 4-5.

Freud, Sigmund (1912a). The Dynamics of Transference. *SE* volume 12, p. 99–108.

Freud, Sigmund (1912b). Ratschläge für den Arzt bei der psychoanalytischen Behandlung. *GW* volume 8, p, 376–387.

Freud, Sigmund (1912c). Recommendations to Physicians Practicing Psycho-Analysis. *SE* volume 12, p. 111–120.

Freud, Sigmund (1914). Remembering, Repeating and Working-Through (Further Recommendations on the Technique of Psychoanalysis, 2). *SE* volume 12, p. 147–156.

Freud, Sigmund (1915a). Observations on Transference-Love (Further Recommendations on the Technique of Psychoanalysis, 3). *SE* volume 12, p. 159–171.

Freud, Sigmund (1915b). The Unconscious. *SE* volume 14, p. 166–204.

Freud, Sigmund (1915c). *Thoughts for the Times on War and Death. SE* volume 14, p. 275–300.

Freud, Sigmund (1919). The Uncanny. *SE* volume 17, p. 219–256.

Freud, Sigmund (1923a). Two Encyclopaedia Articles. *SE* volume 18, p. 235–259.

Freud, Sigmund (1923b). *The Ego and the Id. SE* volume 19, p. 12–59.

Freud, Sigmund (1923c). Neurosis and Psychosis. *SE* volume 19, p. 149–153.

Freud, Sigmund (1924). The Economic Problem of Masochism. *SE* volume 19, p. 159–170.

Green, André (1973). On Negative Capability: A Critical Review of W.R. Bion, *Attention and Interpretation.* Jacqueline Knobil (translator). *The International Journal of Psychoanalysis* (volume 54), p. 115–119.

Green, André (1975). The Analyst, Symbolization and Absence in the Analytic Setting (on Changes in Analytic Practice and Analytic Experience). *The International Journal of Psychoanalysis* (volume 56, part 1), p. 1–22.

Green, André (1979). *The Tragic Effect: The Oedipus Complex in Tragedy.* Frank Kermode (preface). Cambridge: Cambridge University Press.

Green, André (1980a). La mère morte. In *Narcissisme de vie, narcissisme de mort.* Paris: Minuit, 1983, p. 222–253.

Green, André (1980b). The Dead Mother. In *On Private Madness.* Katherine Aubertin (translator). London: Hogarth/Karnac, p. 142–173.

Green, André (1980c). Passions and Their Vicissitudes: On the Relation between Madness and Psychosis. In *On Private Madness.* Katherine Aubertin (translator). London: Hogarth/Karnac, 1997, p. 214–253.

Green, André (1986). *On Private Madness*. London: Hogarth/Karnac, 1997.

Green, André (1993). *Le travail du négatif*. Paris: Minuit.

Green, André (2002). *Idées directrices pour une psychanalyse contemporaine*. Paris: Presses universitaires de France.

Green, André (2011). Le Moment freudien et la théorie kleinienne. Foreword to Christopher Bollas, *Le Moment freudien*. Paris: Ithaque, p. 9–16.

Guntrip, Harry (1968). *Schizoid Phenomena, Object-Relations and the Self*. London: Hogarth and the Institute of Psycho-Analysis.

Harrison, Martin (editor) (2016). *Francis Bacon: Catalogue Raisonné*. London: The Estate of Francis Bacon.

Hécaen, H. and J. de Ajuriaguerra (1952). *Méconnaissances et hallucinations corporelles: intégration et désintégration de la somatognosie*. Paris: Masson.

Heimann, Paula (1950). On Counter-Transference. In *About Children and Children-No-Longer: Collected Papers, 1942–80*. Margaret Tonnesmann (editor). London and New York: Routledge, 1989, p. 73–79.

Heimann, Paula (1980). About Children and Children-No-Longer. In *About Children and Children-No-Longer: Collected Papers, 1942–80*. Margaret Tonnesmann (editor). London and New York: Routledge, 1989, p. 324–343.

Jaron, Steven (2020). Psychoanalysis in the Time of Covid-19. *Psychoanalysis Today*. www.psychoanalysis.today/en-GB/PT-Articles/Jaron-157910/Psychoanalysis-in-the-Time-of-Covid-19.aspx

Jaron, Steven (2021). Katabasis, Anabasis: Working in a Post-ICU Covid Unit in a Public Hospital. In *Psychoanalysis and Covidian Life: Common Distress, Individual Experience*. Howard B. Levine and Ana de Staal (editors). Oxford: Phoenix, p. 203–218.

Jemstedt, Arne (2011). Introduction to *The Christopher Bollas Reader*. Adam Phillips (foreword). London and New York: Routledge, p. xii–xxvii.

Kahn, Laurence (2012). *L'écoute de l'analyste: de l'acte à la forme*. Paris: Presses universitaires de France.

Kahn, Laurence (2017). Actualité de l'hystérie: matrice inconsciente et pulsionnalité selon Christopher Bollas. *Oedipe*. www.oedipe.org/newsletter/20170514/oedipe-info-une-importante-contribution-de-laurence-kahn-au-sujet-du-livre-de-c

Khan, M. Masud R. (1960). Regression and Integration in the Analytic Setting: A Clinical Essay on the Transference and Counter-Transference

Aspects of These Phenomena. In *The Privacy of the Self: Papers on Psychoanalytic Theory and Technique*. London: Hogarth and the Institute of Psycho-Analysis, 1974, p. 136–167.

Kurtág, György (1989–). *Signs, Games and Messages (violin)*. Budapest: Editio Musica Budapest.

Kurtág, György (2009). *Entretiens, textes, dessins*. Geneva: Contrechamps.

Lacan, Jacques (1960). Propos directifs pour un Congrès sur la sexualité féminine. In *Écrits*. Paris: Le Seuil, 1966, p. 725–736.

Lacan, Jacques (1972–73). *Livre XX du Séminaire: Encore*. Jacques-Alain Miller (editor). Paris: Le Seuil.

Laplanche, Jean and J.-B. Pontalis (1964/1985). *Fantasme originaire, fantasme des origines, origines du fantasme*. Paris: Hachette.

Lautréamont, Isidore-Lucien Ducasse (1869). *Les chants de Maldoror. Oeuvres complètes*. Maurice Saillet (editor). Paris: Le Livre de Poche, 1963.

Lichtenstein, Heinz (1977). *The Dilemma of Human Identity*. New York: Aronson.

Melville, Herman (1851). *Moby-Dick: or, the Whale*. Tom Quirk (editor). London: Penguin, 2003.

Milner, Marion (as Joanna Field) (1934). *A Life of One's Own*. Rachel Bowlby (introduction). London and New York: Routledge, 2011.

Milner, Marion (1969). *The Hands of the Living God: An Account of a Psycho-Analytic Treatment*. D.W. Winnicott (foreword). London: Hogarth and the Institute of Psycho-Analysis.

Molino, Anthony (1995). A Conversation with Christopher Bollas. In *The Vitality of Objects: Exploring the Work of Christopher Bollas*. Joseph Scalia (editor) and Malcolm Bowie (preface). Middleton: Wesleyan University Press, 2002, p. 179–222.

Nastasi, Antoine (2016). Les racines corporelles du délire. *Revue française de psychosomatique* (number 50), p. 151–168.

Nettleton, Sarah (2017). *The Metapsychology of Christopher Bollas: An Introduction*. London and New York: Routledge.

Parsons, Michael (2014). An Independent Theory of Clinical Technique. In *Living Psychoanalysis: From Theory to Technique*. London and New York: Routledge, p. 184–204.

Phillips, Adam (2011). Foreword to *The Christopher Bollas Reader*. Arne Jemstedt (introduction). London and New York: Routledge, p. viii–ix.

Pontalis, J.-B. (1984). Argument. *Nouvelle Revue de Psychanalyse* on 'La chose sexuelle.' Christopher Bollas, personal collection.

Pontalis, J.-B. (1990). *La force d'attraction: trois essais de psychanalyse*. Paris: Le Seuil.

Quicherat, L. (1878). *Thesaurus poeticus linguae latinae* (2nd edition). Paris: Hachette.

Rayner, Eric (1991). *The Independent Mind in British Psychoanalysis*. London: Free Association.

Rilke, Rainer Maria (1923). *Duineser Elegien*. Leipzig: Insel.

Rimbaud, Arthur (1873). *Une Saison en enfer. Oeuvres complètes*. Antoine Adam (editor). Paris: Gallimard, 1972, p. 91–117.

Robertson, Paul (2016). *Soundscapes: A Musician's Journey through Life and Death*. London: Faber and Faber.

Schwartz, Murry and Christopher Bollas (1976). The Absence at the Center: Sylvia Plath and Suicide. *Criticism* (volume 18, number 2), p. 147–172.

Searles, Harold F. (1963). The Place of Neutral Therapist Responses in Psychotherapy with the Schizophrenic Patient. In *Collected Papers on Schizophrenia and Related Subjects*. London: Karnac, 1986, p. 626–653.

Sklar, Jonathan (2011). *Landscapes of the Dark: History, Trauma, Psychoanalysis*. Christopher Bollas (introduction). London: Hogarth/Karnac.

Sklar, Jonathan (2017). *Balint Matters: Psychosomatics and the Art of Assessment*. London: Karnac.

Winnicott, D.W. (1954). Metapsychological and Clinical Aspects of Regression within the Psycho-Analytical Set-Up. In *Through Paediatrics to Psychoanalysis: Collected Papers*. London: Hogarth and the Institute of Psycho-Analysis, p. 278–294.

Winnicott, D.W. (1955–56). Clinical Varieties of Transference. In *Through Paediatrics to Psychoanalysis: Collected Papers*. London: Hogarth and the Institute of Psycho-Analysis, p. 295–299.

Winnicott, D.W. (1958). The Capacity to Be Alone. In *The Maturational Processes and the Facilitating Environment*. London: Hogarth and the Institute of Psycho-analysis, p. 29–36.

Winnicott, D.W. (1960). The Theory of the Parent-Infant Relationship. In *The Maturational Process and the Facilitating Environment*. London: Hogarth and the Institute of Psycho-Analysis p. 37–55.

Winnicott, D.W. (1963). Fear of Breakdown. In *Psycho-Analytic Explorations*. Clare Winnicott, Ray Shepherd and Madeleine Davis (editors). Cambridge: Harvard University Press, 1989, p. 87–95.

Winnicott, D.W. (1969). The Use of an Object and Relating Through Identifications. In *Playing and Reality*. London: Tavistock, 1971, p. 86–94.

Winnicott, D.W. (1971). *Playing and Reality*. London: Tavistock.

Wordsworth, William (1805). *The Prelude. The Major Works, Including the Prelude*. Stephen Gill (editor and notes). Oxford: Oxford University Press, 2000, p. 375–590.

Index